Aspects of Britain and the USA

Christopher Garwood
Guglielmo Gardani
Edda Peris

OXFORD UNIVERSITY PRESS

Oxford University Press
Great Clarendon Street, Oxford OX2 6DP

Oxford New York
Athens Auckland Bangkok Bogotá Buenos Aires Calcutta
Cape Town Chennai Dar es Salaam Delhi Florence Hong Kong
Istanbul Karachi Kuala Lumpur Madrid Melbourne Mexico City
Mumbai Nairobi Paris São Paulo Shanghai Singapore Taipei Tokyo
Toronto Warsaw

and associated companies in
Berlin Ibadan

Oxford and Oxford English are trade marks of
Oxford University Press.

ISBN 0 19 454245 9

© Oxford University Press 1992

First published 1992
Ninth impression 2000

The material in this book was first published as Part 3 of
Business and Commercial English by the same authors.

Set by Tradespools, Frome, Somerset

Printed in Hong Kong

Contents

The British people

FACTS AND FIGURES ABOUT THE BRITISH

Exercise 1 In groups, discuss the statistics in the table below. Which statistics surprise you the most? Which aspects of Britain, as shown by the statistics, are similar to those of your country? Which are different?

Statistics that show state of the nation

■ Of the population aged 16 or over in 1987 in England and Wales, 59 per cent were married, 26 per cent single, 9 per cent widowed and 6 per cent divorced. The average age for first marriages was 26 for men and 24 for women.

■ 70 per cent of the 153,000 divorces granted in England and Wales in 1988 were to wives. The average age at which people were divorced was 38 for men and 35 for women.

■ The top 1 per cent of adults own 20 per cent of marketable wealth; the top 10 per cent own 54 per cent.

■ More than 51 per cent of households have two or more television sets. On average those aged over four years spend more than 25 hours a week watching television.

■ Average gross weekly earnings in April 1988 were £241 for full-time male workers and £160 for full-time female workers.

■ At the end of 1987 total US investment in Britain was valued at $45,000m (£277,950m), representing 36 per cent of US investment in the EC.

■ There are 14 distilleries in Scotland which export 84 per cent of their produce. One-fifth of the whisky produced in Britain is drunk in the United States. Britain has 75,000 pubs.

■ The acreage under oil seed rape increased five-fold in the 10 years to 1988.

■ The average daily turnover of London's foreign exchange market was about

£110,000 in 1989, making it the largest such market in the world.

■ Britain has 400 professional arts festivals, 300 theatres, 1,300 cinema screens and 2,400 museums or galleries.

■ About 100 newspapers and magazines are produced by ethnic minorities in Britain.

■ An estimated 5 million people (mainly women) play bingo in commercial bingo halls.

■ About half the households in Britain have a pet, the most common being dogs (of which there are thought to be over 6 million in Britain) and cats, the number of which has gradually risen to about 6 million.

From *The Independent*, 2 January 1990
Information from *Britain 1990: An Official Handbook*, HMSO

Exercise 2 Study the table below and say what changes have occurred in British consumer expenditure. Start by saying: 'The British now spend much less on . . .'

CONSUMERS' EXPENDITURE IN 1978 AND 1988			
	1978	1988	
	per cent	per cent	£ million
Food (household expenditure)	18·2	12·5	36,687
Alcoholic drink	7·2	6·3	18,508
Tobacco	3·9	2·7	7,945
Clothing and footwear	7·8	6·7	19,791
Housing	13·0	14·6	42,993
Fuel and power	4·6	3·9	11,562
Household goods and services	7·5	6·5	19,163
Transport and communications	15·5	17·2	50,398
Recreation, entertainment and education	9·3	8·9	26,096
Other goods and services	13·1	20·6	60,424

Source: *United Kingdom National Accounts 1989 Edition*

Exercise 3 Study the chart below and describe the changes that have occurred in British eating habits. Start by saying: 'The British now eat a little less fresh fruit, but . . .'

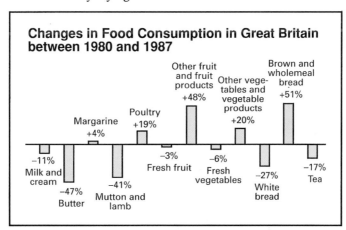

Exercise 4 Study the statistics in the table. Compare the figures for the four countries in the United Kingdom. Compare the figures for the United Kingdom with any figures you know for your country.

	England	Wales	Scotland	Northern Ireland	United Kingdom
Employees in employment ('000, June 1988)	19,252	891	1,928	497	22,568
Unemployment rate (June 1989)	5.7%	8.2%	9.4%	15.3%	6.3%
GDP (per head)	£6,205	£4,991	£5,725	£4,690	£6,052

Source: *United Kingdom National Accounts 1989 Edition*

LEISURE AND SPORT IN BRITAIN

Most people have considerably more free time, more ways in which to spend it and higher real incomes than previous generations. Agreed hours of full-time work are usually from 35 to 40 hours a week, although many people actually work somewhat longer because of voluntary overtime. A large majority of employees work a five-day week.

The most common leisure activities are home based, or social, such as visiting or entertaining relatives or friends. Television viewing is by far the most popular leisure pastime, and nearly all households have a television set, with 90 per cent in 1987 having a colour set. Over 51 per cent of households have two or more television sets and average viewing time for the population aged four and over is 25 hours a week. Growing numbers are using video recorders to watch programmes at times other than their transmission: the proportion of households with a video recorder rose from 24 per cent in 1984 to 46 per cent in 1987. Other popular pursuits include: listening to music, reading, do-it-yourself home improvements, gardening, and going out for a meal or for a drink.

Many people give up free time to work for voluntary organisations, of which there are over 250,000 in England and Wales. It is estimated that about one-quarter of the population is involved in some way in voluntary work in Britain.

Sports and other pastimes have grown in popularity, reflected by increasing membership of the main organisations concerned with outdoor activities, although for some sports, such as greyhound racing, the number of spectators has been declining. Walking and swimming are the two most popular sporting activities, being almost equally undertaken by men and women. Snooker/billiards/pool and darts are the next most popular sports among men. Keep-fit, yoga, squash and cycling are among the sports where participation has been increasing in recent years. The most popular spectator sports are football and rugby in the winter, and cricket and athletics in the summer.

From *Britain 1990: An Official Handbook*, HMSO

Exercise 5   Which activities mentioned above would not appear in a list of leisure activities in your country? What leisure activities in your country are not included here?

Exercise 6   List the sports and pastimes which are . . .

growing in popularity	declining in popularity	most popular as participation sports	most popular as spectator sports

YOUNG PEOPLE IN BRITAIN

Exercise 7   Read the article on the next page. In groups, find out information from the article under these headings:

Attitudes	Habits	Lifestyle
food	buying habits	entertainment
education	languages	
Europe	eating habits	

Youngsters put caring before jobs success

BRITISH youngsters are rejecting the image of the hard-working 1980s yuppie and see themselves as sensitive individuals concerned with the environment, animal testing, and healthy foods, according to report released yesterday.

The 1990s British youngster is "affluent, sensible, caring and unpredictable", says the report, Youth Lifestyles 1990, by the Mintel market research company.

Forty-five per cent of those aged between 20 and 24 who were questioned said they liked to be thought of as "sensible and responsible" while only 16 per cent said they would like to be "up and coming and successful".

Youngsters from lower socio-economic groups are keener to see themselves as "wild and unpredictable".

John Cunningham, chief executive of Mintel, said at yesterday's launch: "The 1980s yuppie label is dead. Today's youngsters are much more open-minded and international."

Almost half the 1,000 15-24 year olds interviewed said they would buy environment-friendly products "provided the price is not too high", and almost the same number said they would not buy products which had been tested on animals.

The number of vegetarians among this age group was almost twice the national average, at 11 per cent. They were most likely to be women, aged 21, from social class AB and living in the South-east.

In education, girls were doing much better than boys with 42 per cent of girls leaving school with O levels or equivalant, compared with 34 per cent of boys.

But, once they are working, girls are more likely to be paid less than boys despite being more highly qualified. In manual jobs, females can, on average, expect to earn £70 a week less than their male counterparts. The disparity in non-manual work is £17.

British youngsters are taking a keen interest in Europe and are more pro-European than the adult population.

More than 68 per cent claimed to know enough of a European language to hold a conversation, with French being the most popular second language.

Almost half said they considered themselves "European" and West Germany was the country in which most would prefer to live.

Siobhan Smith, market analyst for Mintel, said yesterday: "Youngsters are beginning to move away from the boring phase of the 1980s and are getting much more exciting. The yuppie image is on the way out and they are getting much more individualistic."

Most worrying for British employers is the number of youngsters interested in working in another European country: 59 per cent said they would consider this. The figure is greater for those who continued their education beyond 18 and are from higher socio-economic groups.

British youngsters are more likely than their elders to buy foreign goods, especially from Japan. Almost three-quarters of 15 to 19-year-olds and 67 per cent of 20 to 24-year-olds said that working for a Japanese firm would be just as good as working for a British one.

The survey's finding on eating habits reveals a move away from traditional fish and chips. Indian and Chinese restaurants are the most popular among 15 to 19-year-olds, while those aged between 20 and 24 still prefer "traditional English" food.

The rise in popularity of Australian soap dramas and entertainers such as Kylie Minogue has affected youngsters' choice of lifestyle.

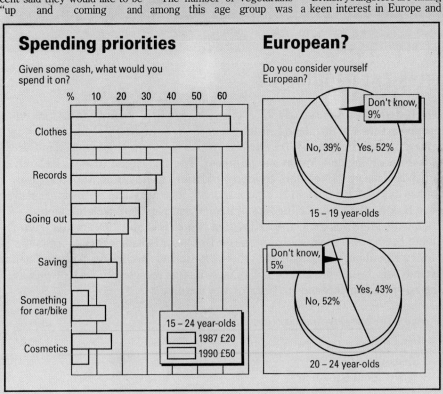

Spending priorities

Given some cash, what would you spend it on?

% 10 20 30 40 50 60

- Clothes
- Records
- Going out
- Saving
- Something for car/bike
- Cosmetics

15 – 24 year-olds
1987 £20
1990 £50

European?

Do you consider yourself European?

Don't know, 9%
No, 39% Yes, 52%

15 – 19 year-olds

Don't know, 5%
No, 52% Yes, 43%

20 – 24 year-olds

From *The Guardian*, 12 July 1990

Exercise 8 What surprises you about the information given about young people in Britain in this article? What similarities and what differences are there between young people in Britain and young people in your country?

The geography of Britain

PHYSICAL GEOGRAPHY

The **British Isles** is the geographical term for a group of about 5,000 islands off the north-west coast of mainland Europe between the latitudes 50°N and 61°N. The largest island is **Britain** or **Great Britain**, which is also the largest island in Europe. It consists of **England**, **Wales** and **Scotland**. The next largest island is **Ireland**, which is made up of **Northern Ireland** (or **Ulster**) and the **Irish Republic** (also known as **Eire**). Britain and Northern Ireland, together with a number of small islands, form the **United Kingdom of Britain and Northern Ireland**, more commonly known as the **United Kingdom** (which is almost 20% smaller than Italy). In everyday usage, however, Great Britain or Britain is used to mean the United Kingdom. The **Isle of Man**, between Ireland and Britain, and the **Channel Islands**, off the north-west coast of France, though recognizing the Crown, have their own parliaments and are largely self-governing.

Exercise 1

1 Match the terms with their correct definitions.

   1 The British Isles
   2 Britain
   3 The United Kingdom

   ☐ England, Scotland and Wales

   ☐ A group of islands including Britain and Ireland

   ☐ England, Scotland, Wales, Northern Ireland and a number of small islands

2 What is the difference between Eire and Ireland?

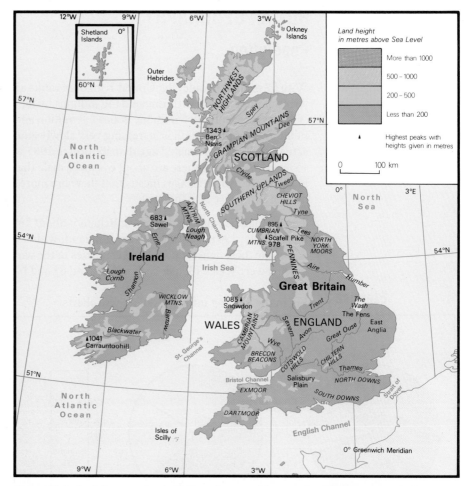

Great Britain is just under 1,000 km long and just under 500 km across in its widest part. The most mountainous region is **Scotland** (with Britain's highest peak, **Ben Nevis** – 1,343 m), which also has a wide lowland area between the Grampians and the Southern Uplands, where most of the large towns, including Edinburgh and Glasgow, and three-quarters of the population are located. Much of **Wales** is also mountainous and in England the **Pennine Range** (the 'backbone of England') extends 224 km (although the highest peak is only 895 m high). The rest of England tends to be rather undulating, and not even the large agricultural plains of **East Anglia** are perfectly flat. In **Ireland** all the highland areas are around the edge, but there are no peaks over 1,100 m.

Rivers in Great Britain are quite short – the longest rivers are the Severn and the Thames – but their easy navigability has made them an important part of the inland transport network for the transportation of bulk products such as coal, iron ore and steel.

Exercise 2   Complete the table.

Highest mountain	....
Longest mountain range	....
Flattest area	....
Longest rivers	....

HUMAN GEOGRAPHY

Population

With **57 million** people, the United Kingdom ranks about fifteenth in the world in terms of population, with England (46 million) by far the most populous part (followed by Scotland 5 million, Wales 2.8 million and Northern Ireland 1.5 million). The population is increasing very slowly and in 1976–78 and 1982 actually fell. The estimated **age distribution** in 1985 was 21%<16; 64% 16–64; 15%>64. Although there are about 6% more male than female births, the higher mortality of men at all ages means that there are more females than males (29 million as against 27.6 million).

The average **population density** in Britain is about 239 per sq.km, compared with, for example, 190 per sq.km in Italy. England, with 361 inhabitants per sq.km, is one of the most densely populated countries in the world (the rest of Britain is much lower: Wales 135 per sq.km, Scotland 65 and Northern Ireland 111).

Exercise 3 Fill in the missing information in these charts.

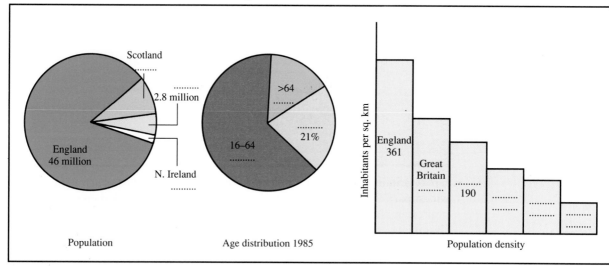

Conurbations and New Towns

The highest densities are to be found in **conurbations** (see the black areas on the map), which are groups of once separate towns that have grown to form a single community. Although Britain is short of housing, planners like to keep a belt of undeveloped land around cities known as a **green belt** to reduce pollution and provide open spaces for leisure. This has meant that the only alternative to the redevelopment of slum areas in the conurbations (such as the Docklands development in London) has been the creation of **New Towns** such as Harlow in Essex. The industrial area in these purpose-built towns is separate from housing and there are more green, open spaces. New Towns have partially failed, however, especially since many are near enough to conurbations for people to use them as **dormitory towns** (towns where a large percentage of the population commutes daily to work in a conurbation) and recent government policy has been to expand existing towns like Telford and Milton Keynes (formed from the amalgamation of a group of villages), which is cheaper than creating an entirely new town.

Exercise 4 Match the terms with their correct definitions.

1 conurbations
2 dormitory towns
3 green belt
4 new towns

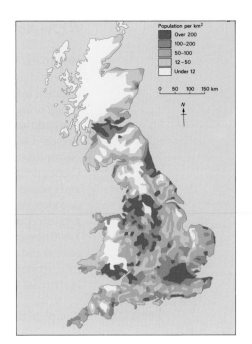

☐ towns built in accordance with the principles of town planning so that their various functions are related to one another in the most efficient and satisfying manner

☐ groupings of towns that were formerly separate, forming single large communities

☐ towns in which people live, but do not work

☐ area of parks and farmland encircling an urban area and protected from development

Exercise 5
1 Name the main conurbations in Britain.
2 What are the advantages of new towns?
3 Why have they not been completely successful?

Ethnic and national minorities

People have been coming to settle in Britain for centuries from many parts of the world. Some came to avoid political or religious persecution, others to find a better way of life or an escape from poverty.

The Irish have long made homes in Britain. Many Jewish refugees started a new life in the country towards the end of the nineteenth century and in the 1930s' and after 1945 large numbers of other European refugees settled in Britain. The large communities from the West Indies and South Asian sub-continent date principally from the 1950s and 1960s. There are also sizeable groups from the United States and Canada, as well as Australians, Chinese and various European communities such as Greek and Turkish Cypriots, Italians and Spaniards. More recently Ugandan Asians and people from Latin America, Indo-China and Sri Lanka have sought refuge in Britain.

In 1985-87, according to the results of a sample survey, the non-white population of Great Britain was about 2.4 million (some 4.5 per cent of the total population), of whom about 43 per cent were born in Britain; one in three was aged under 16 and about one in six aged 45 or over. Although members of the non-white population are disproportionately concentrated in the areas of greatest deprivation in the inner cities, where the disadvantages they share with the poorer sections of the indigenous community are compounded by racial discrimination, progress has undoubtedly been made over the last 20 years in several areas of life. Many individuals have achieved distinction in their careers and in public life and the proportion of ethnic minority workers in professional and managerial jobs has increased. There are at present three black Members of Parliament and one Asian Member of Parliament and the number of ethnic minority councillors in local government is growing.

Notting Hill Carnival, Britain's biggest ethnic festival

From *Britain 1990: An Official Handbook*, HMSO

Exercise 6
1 List the periods in which the majority of immigrants came to Britain.
2 Find out the reasons why they emigrated to Britain.
3 What percentage of the non-white population in Britain are immigrants?
4 Where does the majority of the non-white population in Britain live?

WEATHER AND CLIMATE

Britain has a generally mild, temperate **climate**. The **weather**, however, tends to be very changeable (though not necessarily unpredictable) as a result of the constant influence of different air masses. The prevailing winds are south-westerly, which bring warm air in from across the Atlantic. There are few extremes in **temperature**, which rarely goes above 32°C or below −10°C. In summer, southern Britain is warmer than northern Britain because of its latitude, but in winter the North Atlantic Drift – a warm sea current – keeps the west milder than the east. Consequently Wales and the south-west peninsula have the most moderate climate and eastern England the most extreme. These differences are not great, however, and local variations arising from factors such as altitude and pollution are often greater. Annual **rainfall** is fairly evenly distributed, but ranges from more than 1,600 mm in the mountainous areas of the west and north to less than 800 mm over central and eastern parts. This is because depressions from the Atlantic bring frontal rainfall first to the west and because western Britain is higher and so gets more relief rain.

Exercise 7   Complete the table.

Weather features	Causes
1 very changeable weather	....
2 few extremes in temperature	....
3 South warmer than North	....
4 West milder than East	....
5 frequent local variations	....
6 West wetter than East	....

Exercise 8   Match the weather forecast with the correct chart. Then write a weather forecast for the other chart.

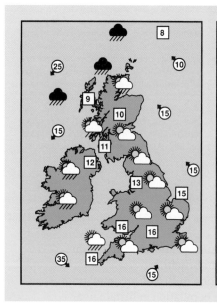 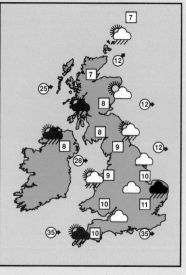

Cloud with a little rain will persist over south-eastern parts of England, but there will be sunny spells over much of the country. Showers will extend from the north west through western areas of Scotland and Northern Ireland. Some of these showers will be heavy and blustery on west-facing coasts. Temperatures will be quite mild for January, with a minimum of 7 degrees Celsius in northern Scotland and a maximum of 11 degrees Celsius in south-east England, but there will be a strong westerly wind with gales in the far south-west.

The geography of Britain

ENERGY AND NATURAL RESOURCES

A fixed oil production platform in the North Sea

Offshore **natural gas**, which is distributed through 5,600km of high-pressure pipelines, is used by industries which require a fine degree of accuracy, but, because it is easily transportable, it has not created industrial areas in the way coal did. About half of the national consumption is used for industrial and commercial purposes, and the remainder for household use. The industry was sold back to the private sector as British Gas Plc in 1986.

Britain is the world's fifth largest **oil producer** and, although production is expected to start declining slowly, Britain should remain a significant producer in the twenty-first century. About 80% of offshore production is brought ashore by submarine pipeline to one of the 14 refineries. There are also a series of onshore pipelines which carry refined products to major marketing areas.

The main consumers of Britain's declining **coal industry**, which still has considerable reserves, are the thermal power stations, which in 1988 accounted for 73% of total consumption to produce roughly one-third of Britain's electricity. Only 10% was used by domestic users.

Britain was the first country in the world to have a public supply of **electricity**, but at the time of writing the industry is in the process of being privatized. The Central Electricity Generating Board (CEGB), which was responsible for generating electricity in England and Wales and for maintaining the national grid, has been split into three companies: PowerGen, National Power, and a national grid company. The twelve regional electricity boards, which are responsible for the distribution and sales of electricity, are being privatized as twelve supply companies. A similar process is happening in Scotland and Northern Ireland. In 1988 domestic users accounted for 35% of the electricity sold, industry 36%, and commercial and other users the rest.

Exercise 9 Complete these diagrams.

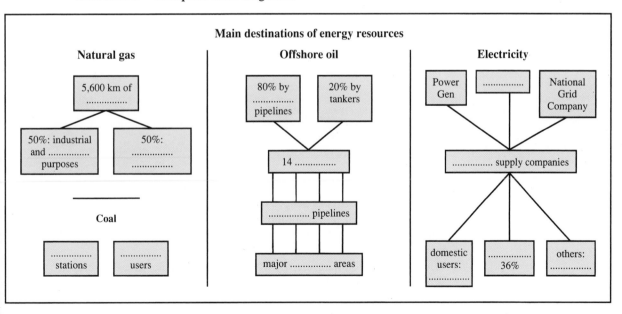

The slow death of nuclear power

The government is not to privatise nuclear power. **Sean O'Neill** reflects on this embarrassing U-turn

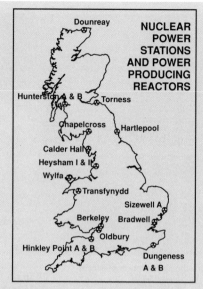

NUCLEAR POWER STATIONS AND POWER PRODUCING REACTORS

Dounreay
Hunterston A & B
Torness
Chapelcross
Hartlepool
Calder Hall
Heysham I & II
Wylfa
Transfynydd
Sizewell A
Berkeley
Bradwell
Oldbury
Hinkley Point A & B
Dungeness A & B

The distribution of nuclear power stations in Britain

BRITAIN'S GREENS are celebrating. They believe the nuclear age is coming to an end.

The government has decided not to include British nuclear power stations in the privatisation of the electricity industry, and it has dropped plans to build three new nuclear power plants costing £6 billion. Furthermore, a government energy forecast predicts that by 2020 nuclear power will be a largely spent force, with the nation using less than it does.

This all amounts to a major U-turn by Mrs Thatcher who has been a strong supporter of the nuclear industry.

Britain has 18 nuclear power stations providing 17 per cent of the country's electricity. Sizewell B, a new pressurized water reactor, will start producing electricity in 1994.

But nuclear power is costly. The electricity it produces is three times more expensive than power from a station burning fossil fuels such as coal and oil. At the end of their active lives, nuclear power plants cost much more to dismantle safely than they do to build.

Unhappiness in the City, where nuclear power was viewed as a high cost, high risk industry, threatened the success of the electricity industry on the stock market. Public confidence in the safety of nuclear power has also been hit hard.

"I think Chernobyl was the turning point in shifting public opinion against nuclear power," says John May, author of *The Greenpeace Book of the Nuclear Age*. "What happened there disproved all the claims that nuclear power was safe."

Other countries have cut back their use of nuclear power as well. In the USA no new reactors have been built since the nuclear accident at Three Mile Island in 1979. Since the Chernobyl disaster in 1986, 20 nuclear plants ordered or under construction in the USSR have been cancelled.

In Australia, Austria, Denmark, Greece, Ireland, New Zealand, Portugal, the Philippines and Norway, governments have adopted non-nuclear policies.

This is the beginning of the end of nuclear power in Britain and the beginning of the end of the nuclear age

"Even if everything was closed down tomorrow we would still be living with the legacy of nuclear power for the next 500 years. No nation has yet solved the problem of what to do with nuclear waste," claims John May.

Greenpeace want to develop environmentally-friendly ways of producing electricity: harnessing the power of the wind, waves, rivers and using "geothermal energy" from deep within the earth.

But the nuclear industry is still powerful. The Department of Energy maintains that nuclear power stations will still be important in supplying electricity. Sizewell B, when it is completed, will be able to generate power for 40 years.

John Collier, chairman of the Atomic Energy Authority, has been chosen to head the new organisation that will run Britain's nuclear power stations after the rest of the electricity industry is sold off. Mr Collier says safety will be his "absolute priority".

He adds: "we have to demonstrate that nuclear power is not only safe but also economic in this country, just as it is elsewhere in the world."

Environmentalists believe that the task is impossible. "This is the beginning of the end of nuclear power in Britain and the beginning of the end of the nuclear age," says John May. "This month has seen the breaching of the Berlin Wall. The Cold War is over. We must ask ourselves now why we need nuclear weapons as well. I think we are entering a whole new era."

From *The Indy*, 23 November 1989

Exercise 10

1 Why do Britain's Greens believe the nuclear age is coming to an end?

2 How many nuclear power stations are there in Britain?

3 Can you see any significance in the location of nuclear power stations as shown by the map?

4 What ways of producing energy would Greenpeace like to see developed?

5 What arguments are there in the article against nuclear power? Can you think of other arguments against it? Can you think of arguments for it?

TRANSPORT AND COMMUNICATIONS

Freight traffic in Britain is carried mainly by road. 82% of the tonnage of inland freight is carried on the roads. The car is also the most popular form of passenger transport, with car and taxi travel accounting for some 82% of passenger mileage within Britain. Railways, inland waterways, coastal shipping and pipelines are important in carrying certain types of freight, particularly bulk goods.

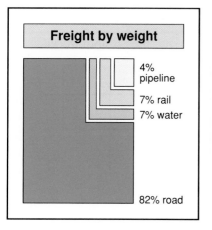

Freight by weight

4% pipeline
7% rail
7% water
82% road

Exercise 11   Comment on the graph. Start by saying: 'The vast majority of freight is . . .'

Roads

Less than 1% of Britain's roads are **motorways** (which are free in Britain), although they carry nearly 13% of traffic including 16% of heavy goods vehicle traffic. Indeed, the network of motorways is inadequate for the volume of traffic and there are terrible congestion problems, especially in and around London.

Britain's motorways and major ports

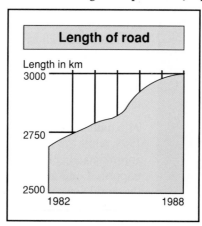

Length of road

Length in km
3000
2750
2500
1982   1988

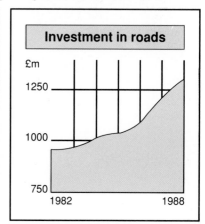

Investment in roads

£m
1250
1000
750
1982   1988

Exercise 12   Comment on the two graphs on the roads, using the information in the text.

Railways

Britain had the world's first public passenger **railway service** (opened in 1825). The various regional railways that developed were nationalized in 1947 and the passenger network now comprises a fast inter-city network (up to 200 km. per hour) linking the main centres of Great Britain; local stopping services; and commuter services in and around large conurbations, especially London. The main freight carried by train is coal, steel and other bulk goods.

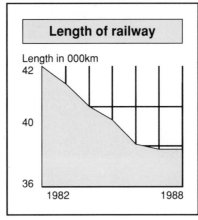

Length of railway

Length in 000km

42

40

36

1982   1988

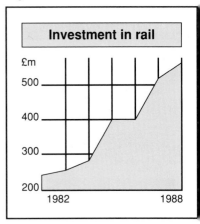

Investment in rail

£m

500

400

300

200

1982   1988

Exercise 13 Comment on the two graphs on the railways. Compare them with the two graphs on roads on the previous page.

Ports and air traffic

Container handling in the Port of London

Almost two-thirds of the traffic through the **ports** is in fuels (mainly petroleum and petroleum products). Traditional major ports like London, Liverpool and Manchester, have lost general (non-bulk) cargo traffic to ports like Dover and Felixstowe, which have developed specialized facilities to meet a world-wide switch from conventional handling methods to container and roll-on modes. Ports on the south and east coasts have also gained traffic as Britain's trade has switched towards the continent of Europe.

94.6 million passengers travelled by air to or from Britain in 1988, while the value of overseas trade carried by air was approximately 21.5% of the value of exports and 16.8% of imports. London's two **airports**, Heathrow and Gatwick, are the world's two busiest airports, mainly as a result of their geographical position.

Exercise 14 1 What kind of freight is carried by sea?
2 Give reasons why traditional ports have declined in importance.
3 Why are Heathrow and Gatwick so important?

NATIONAL PRODUCTION

Membership of the European Community has had a major impact on Britain's pattern of trade. The proportion of Britain's **exports** of goods going to other EC countries has risen to around 50%, while that going to other Commonwealth countries has fallen to around 10%. In recent years, Britain has had a negative balance of trade as regards visible exports and imports, though the balance as regards invisibles is better.

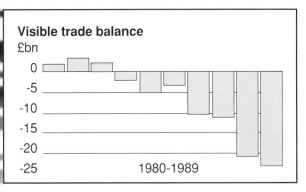

Visible trade balance
£bn
1980-1989

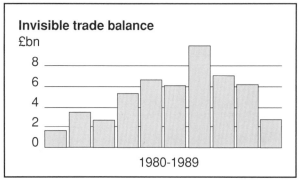

Invisible trade balance
£bn
1980-1989

Exercise 15 Comment on the graphs showing the UK's visible and invisible trade balances.

Industry

Flexible electronic circuits are examined on a lightbox before despatch

Among the main trends in industrial activity in Britain during the 1970s and 1980s have been the decline in **heavy industry** and the growth of the offshore **oil and gas industries** together with related products and services; the rapid development of **electronic and microelectronic technologies** and their application to a wide range of other sectors; and a continuous rise in the **service** (or tertiary) **industries'** share of total employment. **Tourism**, for example, is now one of Britain's most important industries and a growing source of employment (supporting an estimated 1 million jobs in 1985).

In certain regions, older industries, such as coal, steel, shipbuilding and textiles, have steadily declined. As a result **unemployment** is far higher in Scotland, Wales, Northern Ireland and the north of England. The Government has therefore provided various incentives to encourage industrial development in 'assisted areas'.

Exercise 16 Complete the table.

Declining industries	Growing industries
1	1 ....
2	2 ....
3	3 ....
4	4 ....

Privatization

In addition to these structural changes there have also been important changes in ownership. The Thatcher Government returned many of the **nationalized** industries, such as British Airways, British Gas and British Telecom, to the **private sector**, although other industries in the same sectors, such as British Rail, British Coal and the Post Office, are still publicly owned. There has also been a growing trend towards the formation of massive **international corporations** through mergers and acquisitions.

Britain's 10 largest companies			Turnover	Capital employed	Net profit before interest and tax	No. of employees
Rank	Company Name	Main activity				
1	British Petroleum Company	Oil industry	34,932,000	18,477,000	3,883,000	126,400
2	Shell Transport & Trading	Oil industry	23,924,000	14,579,000	2,576,000	N/A
3	B.A.T. Industries	Tobacco, retailing, paper, financial services	11,255,000	6,396,000	1,542,000	168,949
4	Imperial Chemical Industries	Petrochemicals, pharmaceuticals, etc.	11,123,000	6,154,000	1,574,000	127,800
5	Electricity Council	Electricity suppliers	11,118,000	38,777,600	803,500	131,891
6	British Telecommunications	Telecommunication services	10,185,000	12,064,000	2,661,000	235,633
7	British Gas	Gas suppliers, etc.	7,610,000	7,392,000	1,398,000	88,469
8	Hanson	Consumer products, etc.	6,682,000	4,871,000	1,041,000	88,000
9	Shell U.K.	Oil industry	6,677,000	3,685,000	1,087,000	13,636
10	Grand Metropolitan	Hotel props, milk prds., brewers, etc.	5,705,500	3,356,500	586,100	129,436

Exercise 17   Of the 10 largest industrial companies . . .

1 How many were privatized by Mrs Thatcher?
2 In which sector do the majority operate?

Agriculture, fisheries and forestry

Less than 3% of the working population (around 690,000 people) is employed in agriculture in Britain, yet the industry produces nearly two-thirds of Britain's food requirements, with gross output accounting for about 4% of the country's GDP. Just over three-quarters of the land in Britain is used for agriculture. About three-fifths of full-time farms are devoted to **dairying** or **beef cattle** and **sheep**. The majority of sheep and cattle are reared in the hill and moorland areas of Scotland, Wales, Northern Ireland and south-western England, although beef fattening takes place in better grassland areas and arable farms. The farms devoted primarily to **arable crops** are found mainly in eastern and central southern England. **Pig production** occurs in most areas, but is particularly important in eastern and northern England. Britain is also broadly self-sufficient in **poultry meat** and **eggs**.

Britain is one of Europe's most important fishing nations. The **fishing industry** provides about 66% of British fish supplies and it is an important source of employment (16,150 fishermen in regular employment) and income in a number of ports.

Woodland covers an estimated 2.1 million hectares in Great Britain, but the rate of new planting – especially by private owners – is growing and home **timber production** is expected to double over the next 20 years (at present it provides only 10% of the nation's requirements).

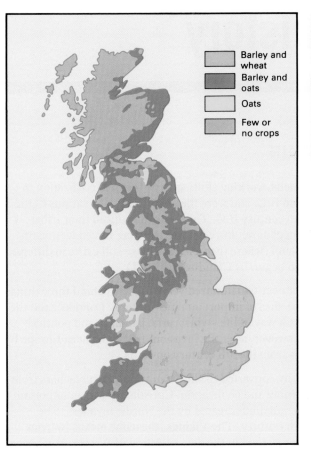

Barley and wheat
Barley and oats
Oats
Few or no crops

Harvesting wheat in East Anglia

Exercise 18 Mark on the map the most important regions for:

- sheep
- cattle
- pigs

Exercise 19 1 Which bar in the graph corresponds to:

- agriculture?
- fish?
- timber?

2 Give the percentages for each industry.

3 Comment on the finished graph. Start like this: 'While the UK is almost self-sufficient as regards fish supplies, producing about 66% of its needs, . . .'

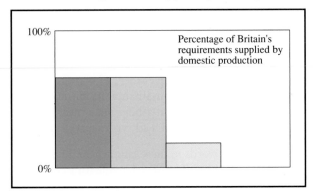

100%

Percentage of Britain's requirements supplied by domestic production

0%

The geography of Britain

British history

An Anglo-Saxon helmet

Third-century Roman floor
mosaic, Fishbourne, Sussex

A Viking longship

PRE-NORMAN BRITAIN

The **Iberians** brought their metal-working skills and the first real civilization to
Britain in the third millennium B.C. and were then overrun by the various Celtic
invasions that began in the 8th century B.C. The **Celts** introduced their tribal
organization and an early form of agriculture before they were forced westwards
into Cornwall, Wales and Ireland (where the Celtic language still exists in different
forms) by the Roman invasion begun by Claudius in 43 A.D.

The **Romans** ruled Britain for over two hundred years and left behind three things
of importance: their roads, the sites of important cities (notably London), and the
seeds of Christianity. The Latin way of life – villas, arts, language and political
organization – all vanished, however, after the invasions from Northern Europe by
the **Angles**, **Saxons** and **Jutes** from the 5th century onwards.

These pagan peoples were easily converted to Christianity and the preachers from
Rome brought with them learning and civilization. Christianity was an important
factor in enabling the various kingdoms created by the Nordic invaders to be
united under Egbert in the 9th century. The **Vikings** (the name means 'warrior')
first raided England to plunder it, then in the days of Alfred of Wessex they began
'to win wide lands to plough and to rule'. In the 10th century England fell under
Danish rule, with King Canute finally managing to unite the **Anglo-Saxons** and
Danes at the beginning of 11th century.

Exercise 1 Complete this chart.

People	Dates	Characteristics/achievements
1 *Iberians*	*3000 B.C.*	*metal working, first real civilization*
2	....	....
3	....	....
4	....	....
5	....	....

Exercise 2 The Celtic language exists today in the form of Scottish Gaelic, Irish Gaelic and
Welsh. Here is same phrase in four languages:

English	Our Father, who art in Heaven . . .
Scottish Gaelic	Ar n-athair a tha air nèamh . . .
Irish Gaelic	Ár n-atheir, atá ar neamh . . .
Welsh	Ein Tad, yr hwn wyt yn y nefoedd . . .

Do you know any words in these languages? The Scottish name for a lake? The
Irish name for Dublin? The Welsh name for a competition of dancing, singing and
poetry?

MEDIEVAL ENGLAND

After defeating the Anglo-Saxon king Harold at the Battle of Hastings in 1066, William of Normandy introduced the Norman **feudal system**, rewarding his French-speaking followers with land in return for their continued support, and French remained the language of the upper classes and administration until the 14th century.

The power of these Norman **Barons** gradually increased and during the reign of the Plantagenets began, together with the Church, to challenge the King's absolute power, which resulted in King John being forced to sign the **Magna Carta** at Runnymede in 1215. This document contained a long list of limitations to the King's power and these rights obtained by the Barons were eventually extended to the entire population.

The origins of **Parliament** are to be found in the reign of John's successor, Henry III. It was a meeting of the King and his Barons and servants at which various administrative and financial problems were discussed. In order to make it easier to put the decisions taken into practice, each Shire had to elect a number of knights to attend these meetings and report the decisions to their Shires. Edward I continued this experiment and in 1295 called a parliament that became known as the **Model Parliament**, at which barons, earls and the high clergy (bishops and abbots) were present, together with the knights and burgesses representing the shires and boroughs. The 'House of Commons' as a separate Chamber resulted from the unofficial meetings of these knights and burgesses. The person chosen to 'speak' for these 'commoners' in Parliament became known as the Speaker.

The Peasants' Revolt

The **Hundred Years' War** fought between France and England had a devastating effect on the English economy. The high taxation necessary to finance the war and the **Black Death** (a plague in 1348 that killed a third of the population of England) led to such extreme hardship for the peasant class that there was a revolt in 1381. Although the **Peasants' Revolt** was soon put down, it led to greatly improved conditions for the peasant class and was the first step towards the ending of the feudal system in England.

Exercise 3   Perhaps the most important of the clauses of the Magna Carta is the one which states that:

'no freeman shall be arrested or imprisoned or disseised [dispossessed] or outlawed or exiled or in any way victimized . . . except by the lawful judgment of his peers or the law of the land'

What constitutional principle is contained in this clause?

Exercise 4   Outline the main characteristics of:

1 the Norman Conquest
2 the Magna Carta
3 the first parliaments
4 the Black Death
5 the Peasants' Revolt

TUDOR ENGLAND

No sooner was the Hundred Years' War over than a long power struggle (1455–85) began for the English Crown between two families: the House of Lancaster and the House of York. The **War of the Roses** (so called because both families used a rose as their symbol) ended when **Henry VII (Henry of Tudor)** united the two rival houses, giving origin to the Tudor dynasty.

During Henry's reign the medieval period came to a close. Men were no longer tied to manors and estates in the country; the power of the towns, with their educated and industrious **middle classes**, began to make itself felt; and there was a revival, or **Renaissance**, of learning, partly as a result of the printing press, which ended the Church's monopoly of learning.

Henry's son and heir, **Henry VIII** (1509–1547), was a typical Renaissance prince: handsome, learned, ambitious and unscrupulous. He also had an instinctive understanding of his times. It was his creation of the Royal Navy that enabled England to realize her imperialistic ambitions under Elizabeth and defy the Pope and the Catholic powers of Europe.

Henry used Parliament to establish himself as the head of the Protestant Church of England with the **Act of Supremacy** in 1534. His decision to act through Parliament greatly strengthened this institution, which had lost virtually all its authority under Henry VII. There was general support on the part of the English people, who were resentful of papal interference in national affairs. His **Reformation** led to the creation of the religiously distinct Anglican Church. The **dissolution of the monasteries** (and the confiscation of their large estates) served to destroy papal authority in England and at the same time provide Henry with much needed wealth.

Elizabeth I (1558–1603) was an outstanding ruler. She restored national unity, opposing extremist doctrines and supporting a moderate form of Protestantism similar to that of her father's. Her reign is considered by many as the **Golden Age** of English history, producing not only poets of the stature of Shakespeare and Spenser, but also prosperity for the entire nation. The discovery of America placed Britain at the centre of the world's trading routes and brilliant naval commanders (especially Sir Francis Drake and Sir Walter Raleigh) enabled England to dominate these trade routes. During this period great trading companies, like the East India Company, were also established. Parliament was regularly called and consulted, while Justices of the Peace administered justice and carried out all the ordinary functions of local government.

Exercise 5 Discuss briefly the following:

1 Social change during Henry VII's reign
2 The role of Parliament under the Tudors
3 The Church in Tudor times
4 The Navy and overseas expansion

THE CONFLICT BETWEEN KING AND PARLIAMENT

The Civil War

Oliver Cromwell

Convinced of the **divine right of kings**, the Stuart kings James I and Charles I followed the medieval notion of monarchy, ignoring Parliament. Charles I raised taxes without its permission and prevented it from meeting for 11 years until he needed its help to raise the money to fight the war against Scotland. Relations between King and Parliament became so bad that civil war eventually broke out (1642).

The majority of the nobles supported Charles and the majority of the gentry supported Parliament in this fight over who should have sovereign power. After **Oliver Cromwell** had led the Parliamentarian Roundheads to victory (1648), Charles I was executed for treason and Cromwell became Lord Protector. England was now a **Republic**.

Exercise 6 Complete the following sentences to obtain a summary of the text.

1 The Stuart kings ignored Parliament because . . .
2 Charles I did not summon Parliament until . . .
3 The Civil War was really a battle to decide . . .
4 The monarch was replaced by . . .

The Levellers

An important group on Parliament's side were the Levellers, who presented a radical constitutional document which included strict **separation** between the different branches of government – the executive, the legislature, and the judiciary. Here are extracts from that document.

> *We the free People of England ... agree to ascertain our Government, to abolish all arbitrary Power, and to set bounds and limits both to our Supreme, and all Subordinate Authority, and remove all known Grievances.*
>
> *And accordingly do declare and publish to the world,*
> *that we are agreed as followeth*
>
> *That the Supreme Authority of England and the territories therewith incorporate, shall be and reside henceforward in a Representative of the people consisting of four hundred persons, but no more; in the choice of whom (according to natural right) all men of the age of one and twenty years and upwards (not being servants, or receiving alms, or having served the late King in arms), shall have their voices ...*
>
> *That two hundred of the four hundred Members, and not less, shall be taken and esteemed for a competent Representative ...*
>
> *That no Member of the present Parliament shall be capable of being elected of the next Representative, nor any member of any future Representative shall be capable of being chosen for the Representative immediately succeeding ...*
>
> *That ... we agree that this present Parliament shall end the first Wednesday in August next 1649 ... and the next Representative may meet and sit in power ... upon the day following, namely the first Thursday of the same August, 1649.*

Exercise 7
1 What was to be the Supreme Authority?
2 Who was allowed to vote?
3 Were Royalist supporters to be prevented from voting?
4 What differences are there between the Levellers' ideas about parliament and the European parliaments of today?

The Restoration of the Monarchy

The monarchy (together with the Anglican Church and the House of Lords) was restored in 1660, two years after Cromwell's death, when Charles II was invited to sit on the throne of a country tired of the harsh morality of Puritan rule. The **Plague**, which killed almost 70,000 of London's inhabitants, and the **Great Fire** (1666), which destroyed most of the city during his reign, were considered signs of God's wrath by the Puritans.

London during the Plague

The Great Fire of London

Although Charles had restored some power to the monarchy by the time James II came to the throne, Parliament's support was necessary to govern the country. Parliament was dominated by two groups: the **Whigs**, who had tried to exclude Charles' Catholic brother from the throne, and the **Tories**, the conservative aristocracy that had favoured the royal prerogative. However, his filling of civil and military posts with Catholics while the Protestants were being murdered in France so angered Parliament that the Tories and Whigs agreed to invite the Protestant William of Orange and Mary (James II's daughter) to take the Crown as joint sovereigns. This **Glorious Revolution** (1688, so-called because it was bloodless) was accompanied by a **Bill of Rights**, which made it obligatory for the sovereign to rule with Parliament's assistance and outlawed Catholicism for all Englishmen, including the King.

Exercise 8   Summarize the passage by answering the following questions.

1 Why was the monarchy restored?
2 What did the King need in order to be able to govern the country?
3 What was the original difference between the Whig and Tory Parties?
4 Why did James II lose the support of the Tories?
5 Why was the Bill of Rights so important?

THE 18TH CENTURY

Under **Queen Anne** Scotland was united with England in 1707 and by the Act of Union their Parliaments became one. Parliament then assumed almost absolute responsibility for running the country during the reigns of **George I** and **George II**, with the king's most influential minister becoming known as the **Prime Minister**. Parliament pursued a vigorous trading policy which led to large areas of Canada and India being colonized at the expense of the French.

Towards the end of this century of the **Enlightenment**, when people felt they could use their reason to dominate both nature and society, some of the most profound political changes in British history occurred and began to shake this belief. They included the traumatic loss of the American colonies in 1776 after a seven-year war and the revolutions in agricultural and industrial methods at home.

The Agricultural Revolution

In the country the open fields with their tiny strips of land worked by peasant farmers were rapidly replaced by compact farms, with large fields enclosed by hedges and ditches to prevent stray animals from ruining the crops or mixing with the new, improved breeds of sheep and cattle. This **agricultural revolution** left large numbers of the rural population landless and destitute, but also led to the massive increase in agricultural production necessary to feed the country's growing non-agricultural population.

Another aspect of the Agricultural Revolution:
improvements in animal breeding

The Industrial Revolution

The **Industrial Revolution** is the name given to the period beginning in the second half of the 18th century in which industry was transformed from hand-work at home to machine-work in factories. The driving force behind this development was the increase in population and the consequent increase in demand for products. This was only made possible, however, by a series of inventions such as the steam-engine.

This change from rural and agrarian to industrial and urban life created serious psychological problems for a formerly rural society based on the family and there were open challenges to the Government by the increasingly organized town and village labourers. The resulting **Reform Bill** of 1832 revealed the force of organized opinion.

Rawsfolds Mill in Yorkshire in 1811; the first mill to install modern machinery

Exercise 9   Describe the main characteristics of:

1 Parliament in the 18th century
2 the Agricultural Revolution
3 the Industrial Revolution

VICTORIAN BRITAIN

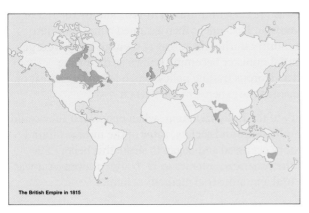

The British Empire in 1815

The British Empire in 1880

During **Queen Victoria**'s sixty-four year reign (1837–1901) the **British Empire**, led by an array of great statesmen and supported by great industrial expansion, grew to a size so vast that 'the sun never sets upon it'. This Empire, whose creation began initially from commercial motives, was also added to for strategic and even missionary reasons and eventually comprised about a quarter of the world's population and land surface. Yet only towards the end of the nineteenth century was there any strong public sentiment in favour of it.

Queen Victoria

A Victorian family, photographed in 1889

Victoria's long reign saw many changes in British institutions and the British 'way of life'. Her practice of insisting on being informed about government policy while remaining politically neutral fixed the position of the **Crown** in the Constitution. Her rejection of the amusements and life of the aristocracy enabled the common people to identify themselves with this simple wife and widow, which led to a revival of popular **support for the monarchy**. Above all, her essentially middle-class views and life-style, combined with the rise of the middle classes themselves, led to an affirmation of values – the paternalistic integrity and discipline of the family, the sobriety and puritanism of public life – which in later years came to be known as '**Victorian values**' to which the Thatcher Government of the 1980s wished to return.

Exercise 10

1 What enabled Britain to create such a vast empire?
2 What were the reasons behind the creation of this empire?
3 In which three ways did Victoria change life in Britain during her reign?

British history

The rise of the working class

An iron foundry

At the same time as the middle classes were expanding in Victorian Britain, so were the working classes. The **Industrial Revolution** had now entered its second stage: new industries were developed, new factories were built, Britain's products were exported all over the world, and Britain became known as 'the workshop of the world'.

Life in the new factories and towns was one of terrible hardship. Men, women and children worked fifteen or sixteen hours a day in dangerous, unhealthy conditions for poor wages and lived in dirty, dreary slums, so vividly described by Charles Dickens in the novel *Bleak House*.

The brickmaker's house was one of a cluster of wretched hovels in a brickfield, with pigsties close to the broken windows, and miserable little gardens before the doors, growing nothing but stagnant pools. Here and there, an old tub was put to catch the droppings of rain-water from a roof or they were banked up with mud into a little pond like a large dirt-pie. At the doors and windows, some men and women lounged or prowled about ...

Mrs Pardiggle, leading the way with a great show of moral determination, and talking with much volubility about the untidy habits of the people, conducted us into a cottage at the farthest corner, the ground-floor room of which we nearly filled. Besides ourselves, there were in this damp offensive room – a woman with a black eye, nursing a poor little gasping baby by the fire: a man, all stained with clay and mud, and looking very dissipated, lying at full length on the ground, smoking a pipe; a powerful young man, fastening a collar on a dog; and a bold girl, doing some kind of washing in very dirty water. They all looked up at us as we came in, and the woman seemed to turn her face towards the fire, as if to hide her bruised eye; nobody gave us any welcome ... 'I want an end to these liberties took with my place,' (growled the man upon the floor). 'You haven't no occasion to be up to it. I'll save you the trouble. Is my daughter a washin? Yes, she is a washin. Look at the water. Smell it! That's wot we drinks. How do you like it, and what do you think of gin, instead! An't my place dirty? Yes, it is dirty – it's nat'rally dirty, and it's nat'rally onwholesome; and we've had five dirty and onwholesome children, as is all dead infants, and so much the better for them, and for us besides.'

Parliament was forced to come to terms with the new social conditions. The **Reform Act** of 1832, which granted the franchise to tenants of land, was followed by other urgently needed **social reforms**: the creation of the police force; free, compulsory education (1870); gradual legal recognition of trade unions; the extension of the vote. First to town labourers (1867) and then to agricultural labourers (1884).

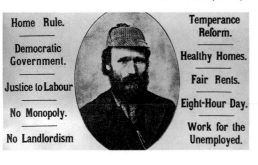

Home Rule.
Democratic Government.
Justice to Labour
No Monopoly.
No Landlordism

Temperance Reform.
Healthy Homes.
Fair Rents.
Eight-Hour Day.
Work for the Unemployed.

Meanwhile the working classes were becoming organized. While the ideas of Karl Marx never won much support among British workers (even though Marx himself studied and wrote most of his works while living in London), the idea of **socialism** was nevertheless a potent force in late Victorian Britain. In the last quarter of the century there was a massive increase in trade unionism and in 1893 the founding of the **Labour Party**, led by Keir Hardie, gave the proletariat a greater voice in Parliament.

Exercise 11

1 Summarize the working and living conditions of the working classes in Britain during the 19th century.
2 Summarize how Parliament reacted to these conditions.
3 Summarize how the working classes themselves reacted.

BRITAIN'S DECLINE AS A WORLD POWER

Victoria's death in 1901 coincided with the beginning of the **decline** in the power of the Empire. The white settler colonies had always enjoyed considerable self-government and in the first decade Canada, Australia, South Africa and New Zealand were all allowed to draw up their own constitutions to become **dominions**. The non-white colonies were not so fortunate: India, 'the jewel in the Crown' of Victoria's Empire, was subjected to an often harsh military rule, and vast areas of Africa remained firmly under British domination.

World War I

Britain was not the only European country with an empire. France, Germany, Belgium, Austria and Hungary were all imperialist powers, and other countries such as Italy also had dreams of empire. British industry no longer enjoyed the total domination of world markets that it had in the 19th century; Germany was rapidly becoming the dominant economic power in Europe.

The rivalry between the great European powers led almost inevitably to the outbreak of **World War I** in 1914. It was the bloodiest war in history. When it ended in 1918 in victory for the Allied Powers of Britain, France, America and Italy, more than 10 million men had been killed. In Britain, the only positive outcome of the war was that women's contribution to the war effort had been so important that it was impossible to deny them the **right to vote** in the 1919 elections.

One of the strangest phenomena of World War I was the wealth of literature and poetry produced by young, upper-class officers serving in the British Army during the war. Read and study one of the most famous of these poems, written in 1914 by Rupert Brooke who died in 1915 while on active service in the Royal Naval Division.

The poet Rupert Brooke

Soldiers in the trenches during World War I

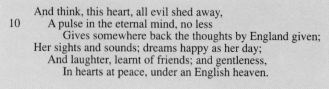

The Soldier

1 If I should die, think only this of me:
    That there's some corner of a foreign field
That is for ever England. There shall be
    In that rich earth a richer dust concealed;
5 A dust whom England bore, shaped, made aware,
    Gave, once, her flowers to love, her ways to roam,
A body of England's, breathing English air,
    Washed by the rivers, blest by suns of home.

And think, this heart, all evil shed away,
10   A pulse in the eternal mind, no less
      Gives somewhere back the thoughts by England given;
Her sights and sounds; dreams happy as her day;
    And laughter, learnt of friends; and gentleness,
      In hearts at peace, under an English heaven.

Exercise 12

1 The first four lines of the poem imagine the death and burial of the soldier. Where?
2 The next four lines recall some of the things the soldier loved about England. What are they?
3 What is the poet's idea contained in lines 9–11 of the poem?
4 Lines 12–14 of the poem recall some more memories of England. What are they?

The years of depression

The war was followed by a period of severe hardship throughout Europe as the depressed economies struggled to recover from the war effort in the face of the expanding American and Asian economies. It was a period of great social unrest and mistrust between the various classes. Unemployment was high, wages low and there were numerous strikes, including a **General Strike** in 1926 by all the unions in an unsuccessful attempt to stop the owners of the coal mines cutting miners' wages.

Mounted police disperse a demonstration in London during the General Strike

In search of work during the Depression

The great **Depression** of the 1930s actually began with the collapse of the American financial markets (the Wall Street crash) in 1929. In Britain unemployment reached huge proportions: over three million people, out of a total workforce of 14 million, were out of work. The formation of a **National Coalition Government**, including Conservative leaders and former Labour Party leaders, proved to be no solution.

Exercise 13 List the main characteristics of the 20s and 30s in Britain.

World War II

Britain was soon involved in another war, for which it was ill-prepared. The Prime Minister Chamberlain had done everything possible to appease Germany (including accepting its occupation of Czechoslovakia) while the country tried to rearm, but Britain and France were still not ready when they declared war on Germany on 3 September 1939 after Hitler's invasion of Poland. As Germany swept through Europe, Britain found herself almost alone and only a courageous effort by her Air Force (prompting Churchill's famous speech: 'Never in the field of human conflict was so much owed by so many to so few') prevented Germany from invading Britain. Germany's subsequent unsuccessful invasion of Russia, together with the intervention of the United States, enabled Britain and her allies to stop Germany once more. The war had cost Britain a quarter of its national wealth.

Exercise 14 Complete the following sentences to obtain a summary of the passage.

1 Britain allowed Germany to invade Czechoslovakia because . . .
2 However, Britain was still unprepared for war when . . .
3 The country was saved by . . .
4 Germany lost the war after . . .
5 For Britain the war had been very . . .

POST-WAR RECONSTRUCTION

Labour's triumph

Minister of Health Aneurin Bevan visits a hospital, 1949

The war was a great class leveller, but it was Labour's offering of a concrete programme as opposed to the ideological worries of Churchill that enabled the party to obtain a massive majority in the 1945 elections. The Labour government, under Prime Minister Clement Attlee, using the planning experience gained during the war, **nationalized** the railways and the coal, steel, shipbuilding, gas and electricity industries, and extended the social services provided by the state to include such things as insurance against unemployment, sickness and old age, a weekly benefit for minimum needs, and free medical health care for everyone (**National Health Service**). This legislation came to be known as the **Welfare State**.

In foreign policy India and Pakistan, together with a number of other former colonies, were finally granted **independence**, as Britain made the painful decision of turning its back on its former Empire to strengthen ties with Europe. The first sign of this was membership of the **North Atlantic Treaty Organization** (**NATO**).

Exercise 15   Give a short description of:

1 nationalization
2 the Welfare State
3 Britain's foreign policy after the war

The affluent society

There then followed a period of economic growth and prosperity under three consecutive Conservative Governments. During the 1950s, there was a period of massive growth in the private sector, above all in the newer industries, particularly car and aircraft production, and wages increased by 40% in real terms. Most families could now afford a car, fridge and a television set, and people began to talk of an **affluent society**. By the start of the 1960s, however, production was beginning to slow, while wages and prices continued to rise. The Government's policy of freezing wages as a cure enabled Labour to win the 1964 elections.

Queen Elizabeth with Commonwealth Prime Ministers, 1960

Abroad, the British Empire had been almost completely dismantled, generally very peacefully, with most of the newly independent nations joining the **Commonwealth**. The decline of Britain as a world power was highlighted, however, when Britain was forced to withdraw its troops in the face of world opposition after occupying the **Suez Canal** (in retaliation for its nationalization by the Egyptian leader Colonel Nasser) and accept the conditions laid down by Egypt.

Exercise 16   Mark the following statements True or False and correct any false statements in order to obtain a summary of the passage.

1 Under the three Conservative governments the economy grew considerably.
2 This growth was caused primarily by the public sector.
3 This period became known as the 'affluent society' because most households were able to buy a car, a TV and a fridge.
4 The Labour Party won the 1964 election because wages continued to rise.
5 Most of the former colonies had to use force to gain their independence.
6 The Suez crisis revealed Britain's decline as a world power.

THE 60s AND 70s

Britain's loss of influence in world affairs was one of the reasons why the newly elected Labour Government supported Britain's application for membership of the **European Economic Community (EEC)**. The main problems faced by the Government were economic, however, and it adopted the severest measures, including **wage freezes** and a 14% **devaluation** of sterling, in an unsuccessful attempt to overcome the difficult economic situation. Numerous strikes and student protests revealed the general social unrest and mistrust in the democratic institutions, and it was little surprise that Labour lost the 1970 election.

Teenagers at Windsor Pop Festival, 1967

The 'Swinging Sixties'

Nevertheless the early 1960s were, for the young people of Britain, a time of great excitement and liberation. Teenagers had jobs, money in their pockets, and the freedom to spend it. They spent it on clothes and entertainment and above all on records. The 'Swinging Sixties', as they came to be known, saw an explosion in the world of pop music and the pop groups of those years – The Beatles, the Rolling Stones – became the heroes of young people not just in Britain but all over the world.

Miners' leaders Joe Gormley and Mick McGahey, 1973

The seventies

The Tory Government of 1970–4, faced by the same problems of a low growth rate, high trade deficits, spiralling inflation and high wage claims backed by numerous strikes, attempted the same cure of a prices and incomes policy. The situation was made impossible, however, by the massive increase in **oil prices** following the Arab-Israeli war and a work-to-rule by the coal-miners in 1973. The country came to an almost complete economic standstill, as electricity could only be supplied to industry for 3 days a week. The only high point in this period of gloom was Britain's entry into the EEC on January 1, 1973 (a decision confirmed 2:1 by the electorate in a subsequent referendum).

After Labour's return to power in 1974, the Government attempted to tackle the severe economic situation through massive cuts in defence spending, but it was not until the **International Monetary Fund** began a rescue operation at the end of 1976 that a dramatic recovery got underway. This recovery was also due to the high levels of **oil** production reached in the **North Sea**.

Exercise 17   During the 1960s and 1970s, Britain was faced by two major problems: its continuing loss of influence in world affairs, and the economy. What solutions were attempted for these problems?

Loss of influence	The economy

BRITAIN AND IRELAND

British **colonization** of Ireland began in the Middle Ages under Henry II, but the real **conquest** of Ireland dates from the beginning of the 17th century, when James I of England began the systematic **expropriation of land** from the Irish by sending anti-Catholic Protestants from Scotland to settle in **Ulster**, the north-eastern region of Ireland which had always put up the greatest resistance to English rule. Fifty years later, Oliver Cromwell put down Irish rebellions with extreme ferocity. In 1690 the Irish made another attempt to resist the conquest of their country by allying themselves with the attempt of James II of England to recover his crown after the 'Glorious Revolution' of 1688 had replaced him with William III. Their defeat, at the **Battle of the Boyne**, gave an ascendancy to the pro-British Protestants which has lasted in Ulster until the present day.

The Irish continued to resist. By the end of the 19th century, most people in Britain favoured **Home Rule** for Ireland, but the Protestant **Unionists** in the north were sufficiently strong to prevent it. In 1916, however, the Irish rebelled once again, when a group of Irish Republicans staged the famous **Easter Rising** in Dublin. The uprising was put down, and the leaders were executed, but the brutal methods used by the British troops strengthened Irish resistance and led to the formation of the **Irish Republican Army (IRA)** which fought for five years against British occupation. This resulted, in 1921, in **independence** being conceded to the 26 counties of southern Ireland (which became the Republic of Eire in 1949).

Ulster, however, was allowed to remain within the United Kingdom. The ruling Unionist politicians in the Ulster Parliament used their power to discriminate against the Catholic minority (about 30% of the population) as regards jobs, housing, and the voting system, and the British government continued to ignore all complaints. The injustices gave rise to a **civil rights movement** among Catholics and Republicans in Northern Ireland in the 1950s, but the stronger it grew the more violent was the reaction of the Ulster unionists.

Eventually, in 1969, the British government sent in the **British Army** to 'restore peace' and safeguard the Catholic minority against the attacks of the Unionists. Greeted at first as 'saviours' by the Catholic population, the British troops soon however came to be regarded as enemies; relations reached their worst point in 1972 on **Bloody Sunday** when British troops fired on a civil rights demonstration in Derry, killing thirteen people.

In reaction to this and other atrocities, the IRA began a military and terrorist campaign against British rule which is still continuing. Since then successive British governments have tried to solve the 'Irish Question' by a variety of political initiatives. This has been impossible to achieve, however, as the great mass of Catholics in Ulster see no solution except re-unification with the Irish Republic, and the vast majority of Protestants violently oppose re-unification on any terms.

Exercise 18

1 List the historical events in relations between Britain and Ireland.
2 List the causes of the troubles in Northern Ireland.
3 Discuss the problem. What possible solution can you offer?

British history

THE THATCHER REVOLUTION

THE Thatcher 'revolution' didn't begin in the '80s — the Iron Lady, as she has been dubbed, was elected Prime Minister in 1979 — but it did dominate the decade.

Political observers from all over the world argue that it has been her single influence and her steadfast commitment to her own form of Conservatism which has been responsible for the nation's dramatic shift in attitudes. A shift, until the advent of the '80s, thought by most people to be impossible.

The grocer's daughter from Grantham — Britain's first woman prime minister — has served more consecutive years in office than any other Prime Minister since 1827.

Throughout the decade she has come through crisis after crisis — many, some would say, of her own making.

In 1982 she faced an invasion of the Falkland Islands — barren lumps of rock in the South Atlantic Ocean — by right wing aggressors from Argentina. In this instance she met force with force, despatching a military Task Force to replant the Union Flag in Port Stanley, the islands' capital.

Britain suffered the harsh effects of a world economic recession, with record unemployment. Battles with the trade unions and rioting in the country's most deprived areas were dealt with in the same way. The year-long miners' strike, starting in 1984, was the high point of a decade of industrial confrontation.

Despite all this, she became even more popular with the electorate, and won the biggest post-war majority in the House of Commons.

Mrs Thatcher once said she wanted Britain to make a return to Victorian values. In many respects the country has.

Most significant is Mrs Thatcher's creation of a new breed of Briton. Seizing upon the driving forces of greed and selfishness Mrs Thatcher has, deliberately or not, appealed to many voters for the simple reason that they feel they have more to gain under Tory rule.

Budgets throughout the '80s have whittled down income tax, and state-owned facilities such as water and British Gas have been handed over to voters along with council houses.

Mrs Thatcher's popularity has been built from people wanting more money in their pockets, more home ownership, more of everything.

Thatcherism gave birth to a society of Filofax and cellular phone-wielding Yuppies, a new class drawn from a cross section of other classes, backgrounds and educations.

The Sixties, they say, was a decade of one long party. The '70s languished in their wake as a kind of hangover. The '80s has been the time when half the nation has woken up, started to feel better, and gone out for another party. The other half of the nation has stayed in — too broke to set foot outside the house.

After a decade of Thatcherism people, overall, ARE better off.

But, some people argue, when Britain has enjoyed such great possessions of knowledge, wealth and communications, why has it still allowed its industry, institutions and world standing to fall to such a low level?

When the need for knowledge has been so great, why have the government's actions been so dire as to result in discouraging young men and women from entering further education?

When the need and support for health, health education and research has been so great—especially since the discovery of the AIDS virus — why has the government's continual battering of the NHS gone on?

When have Britons been so money-grabbing, yet so generous, bearing in mind the successes of Live Aid, Children in Need etc?

Mrs Thatcher has been a great leader — great in terms of achieving what she set out to do. Whether historians will judge her as truly great in terms of furthering Britain's national spirit and identity, only time will tell...

From *Early Times*, 21 December 1989

Exercise 19 1 Why is Mrs Thatcher's period in office considered a 'revolution'?

2 The article contains pros and cons with regard to Mrs Thatcher's period in office. Make a list of the points:

In favour	Against

British institutions

THE CONSTITUTION

The British Constitution is an **unwritten** constitution, not being contained in a single legal document. It is based on **statutes** and important documents (such as the **Magna Carta**), **case law** (decisions taken by courts of law on constitutional matters), **customs** and **conventions**, and can be modified by a simple Act of Parliament like any other law. It contains two main principles – **the rule of law** (i.e. that everyone, whatever his or her station, is subject to the law) and **the supremacy of Parliament**, which implies that there is no body that can declare the activities of Parliament unconstitutional and that Parliament can in theory do whatever it wishes. The constitutional safeguard of the **separation of powers** between **the Legislature** (the two Houses of Parliament), which makes laws, **the Executive** (the Government), which puts laws into effect and plans policy, and **the Judiciary**, which decides on cases arising out of the laws, is only theoretical.

Exercise 1   Complete the following table.

Constitution of the United Kingdom
Main characteristic: ....
Based on: ....
Main principles: ....

Exercise 2   Match the following terms with their correct definition.

1 rule of law
2 separation of powers
3 supremacy of Parliament

☐ There is no legal opposition to Parliament.

☐ Everyone is equal before the law.

☐ Laws are made, put into effect, and interpreted by different bodies.

THE MONARCHY

Britain's Sovereigns from 1066					MARY I	...	...	...	1553–1558
					ELIZABETH I	...	...	...	1558–1603
					JAMES I	...	...	...	1603–1625
					CHARLES I	...	...	...	1625–1649
WILLIAM I	...	...	...	1066–1087	*Commonwealth Declared 1649*				
WILLIAM II	...	...	...	1087–1100	OLIVER CROMWELL				
HENRY I	...	...	...	1100–1135	LORD PROTECTOR		...		1653–1658
STEPHEN	...	...	...	1135–1154	RICHARD CROMWELL				
HENRY II	...	...	...	1154–1189	LORD PROTECTOR				1658–1659
RICHARD I	...	...	...	1189–1199	CHARLES II	...	...	...	1649–1685
JOHN	...	...	...	1199–1216	JAMES II	...	...	...	1685–1689
HENRY III	...	...	...	1216–1272	WILLIAM III			...	1689–1702
EDWARD I	...	...	...	1272–1307	and				
EDWARD II	...	...	...	1307–1327	MARY II			...	1689–1694
EDWARD III	...	...	...	1327–1377	ANNE		...	...	1702–1714
RICHARD II	...	...	...	1377–1399	GEORGE I	...	...	...	1714–1727
HENRY IV	...	...	...	1399–1413	GEORGE II	...	...	...	1727–1760
HENRY V	...	...	...	1413–1422	GEORGE III	...	...	...	1760–1820
HENRY VI	...	...	...	1422–1461	GEORGE IV	...	...	...	1820–1830
EDWARD IV	...	...	...	1461–1483	WILLIAM IV	...	...	...	1830–1837
EDWARD V	...	...	...	1483	VICTORIA	...	...	...	1837–1901
RICHARD III	...	...	...	1483–1485	EDWARD VII	...	...	...	1901–1910
HENRY VII	...	...	...	1485–1509	GEORGE V	...	...	...	1910–1936
HENRY VIII	...	...	...	1509–1547	EDWARD VIII	...	...	...	1936
EDWARD VI	...	...	...	1547–1553	GEORGE VI	...	...	...	1936–1952
JANE GREY	...	...	...	1553	ELIZABETH II	...	...	Succeeded 1952	

The United Kingdom is one of six constitutional monarchies within the European Community and this institution dates back in Britain to the Saxon king Egbert. Since the age of absolute monarchy there has been a gradual decline in the Sovereign's power and, while formally still the head of the **executive** and the **judiciary**, **commander-in-chief** of all the armed forces, and temporal **governor** of the Church of England, nowadays *monarchs reign but they do not rule*.

By statute and convention no monarch may be of Roman Catholic faith, nor marry someone of that faith; and the title to the throne passes to the male line of the family in order of descent and, if there are no sons, to the daughters in order of descent.

Although many people consider the monarchy to be a somewhat **anachronistic** and **undemocratic** institution, the Queen continues to enjoy the support of the vast majority of Britons and she does have certain undeniably useful functions. Besides carrying out important ceremonial duties, she also acts as a 'unifying force' in both the Constitution and the nation, lying outside of the political debate. Moreover, her regular meetings with successive Prime Ministers and personal contacts with numerous foreign leaders mean that she is better informed than most ministers.

Exercise 3 Which of the Queen's functions are formal? Which are real? Which sentence in the passage summarizes the difference between her formal and real powers?

Exercise 4 List and discuss the advantages of monarchies and republics

Monarchies		Republics	
Advantages	Disadvantages	Advantages	Disadvantages

THE LEGISLATURE

Parliament is the supreme legislative authority and consists of three separate elements: the **Sovereign**, the **House of Lords** and the elected **House of Commons**. Over the centuries the balance between the three parts of the legislature has changed, so that the Queen's role is now only formal and the House of Commons has gained supremacy over the House of Lords.

The House of Commons

The House of Commons is a popular assembly elected by almost universal adult suffrage. There are 650 **Members of Parliament** (**MPs**) – each member representing one of the 650 geographical areas (**constituencies**) into which the country is divided for electoral purposes (523 for England, 38 for Wales, 72 for Scotland and 17 for Northern Ireland). If an MP dies, resigns or is made a peer, a **by-election** is held in that constituency to elect a new MP. Leaders of the Government and Opposition sit on the front benches of the Commons, with their supporters (**back-benchers**) behind them. The House is presided over by the **Speaker**.

The main function of the House of Commons is to **legislate**, but the strong party system in Britain has meant that the initiative in government lies not with Parliament but with the Government (most **Bills** are introduced by the Government, although they may also be introduced by individual MPs) and party members almost automatically pass whatever is put before them by their party.

The House of Lords

The House of Lords, which is presided over by the **Lord Chancellor**, is probably the only upper House in the democratic world whose members (1,175 in 1986) are not elected. It is made up of the **Lords Spiritual** and the **Lords Temporal**; the former consist of the representatives of the Church of England (the Archbishops of York and Canterbury and 25 bishops); the latter comprise all **hereditary** and **life peers** (life peers, named by the Sovereign on the advice of the Prime Minister, do not pass on their title when they die). The House of Lords can revise Bills sent to it by the House of Commons but it can only delay a Bill from becoming law for a maximum of 12 months.

Exercise 5   Match the following terms with their definitions.

1 constituency
2 by-election
3 back-bencher

☐ special election held to fill an unexpected vacancy

☐ electoral district

☐ MP who does not hold office in government or opposition

Exercise 6   Complete this diagram.

The Sovereign

House of Commons	House of Lords
.... elected members	.... Archbishops Hereditary Peers
Presided over by:	.... Bishops .... Peers
Main function:	Presided over by: ....
	Main function: ....

Exercise 7   The following article lists the arguments in favour of and against the House of Lords. Read the article and complete the table that follows it.

The House of Lords is back at work next week: some say it should never work again

Aristocrats out!

*The Lords don't represent anybody. Nobody can question what they do. If we, the people, don't like what they get up to we aren't even allowed to vote against them.

*The House of Lords is a dumping ground for failed, old politicians. When you see them on television you would think they're going to fall down and die at any moment. How can they have any idea about what's going on on the streets, in the real world?

*There's no place for all those ancient traditions in modern politics. What's the point of people dressing up in gowns every so often, having that silly old bloke sitting on the Woolsack and grown men calling each other "my noble Lord" all the time?

*Basically the House of Lords is very unfair. Most of those old aristocrats and landowners are Conservatives. So you end up with a permanent Conservative Party majority that can block the policies of a Labour Government in the House of Commons.

My dear fellow ...

*The Lords come from all walks of life. Peerages have been given to Trade Unionists, Clergymen and Industrialists. We represent society as a whole.

*The House of Lords allows some of Britain's most distinguished people, politicians and otherwise, to have a say in how our country is governed. To have former Prime Ministers and experienced figures still helping the country with their knowledge is important.

*The House of Lords is not dominated by old customs. We are prepared to change, indeed we installed television cameras years ago. The House of Commons is only doing that now. The traditions we do continue are important links with our country's heritage.

*It is wrong to say we always agree with the Tory government. Because the government has such a huge majority in the Commons, we are providing the only real opposition by questioning and changing its policies when they come before us.

From *The Indy*, 5 December 1989

Arguments in favour	Arguments against
1	1 ....
2	2 ....
3	3 ....
4	4 ....

THE EXECUTIVE

Prime Minister and Cabinet

Members of the Cabinet, July 1990

The leader of the party which obtains a majority of seats in a **general election** is named **Prime Minister** and is formally asked by the Sovereign to recommend a group of ministers to form a Government. The position of Prime Minister is based on convention, not statute, and dates back to when George I left the running of the country's affairs to his ministers. A number of ministers are invited by the Prime Minister to attend regular meetings to discuss policy and this group of ministers is known as the **Cabinet**. It is a political convention for the Cabinet to act as a single man, which means that a minister who cannot accept a Cabinet decision must resign. (The main opposition party forms a **Shadow Cabinet**, which is more or less as the Government would be if the party were in power, and the relevant members act as opposition spokesmen on major issues.)

Exercise 8   Answer the following questions to obtain a summary of the passage.

1 How is the Prime Minister chosen in Britain?
2 What is the Cabinet?
3 What must a Cabinet Minister do if he/she disagrees with a Government decision?
4 What is the job of a Shadow Minister?

Exercise 9   Is there any difference between the way the Prime Minister is chosen in Britain and in your country? Is the role of the Opposition different in any way?

Powers of Government

The wide powers of patronage held by the Prime Minister and the strong party system, together with certain constitutional hangovers from the past, have given the Government immense power.

The most contentious hangover from the age of absolute monarchy is the Royal Prerogative, surrendered by the Crown in 1688 and given not to Parliament, but to ministers and Whitehall. It has left Parliament weaker than it was before the "Glorious Revolution" for although monarchs had more power and authority before, they still had to go to Parliament for money for their secret services, for example, or for funds to make war. Professor John Griffith, Emeritus Professor of Public Law at the London School of Economics, has said:

"Despite the great constitutional changes that have taken place between the period of the first Elizabeth and today, the struggle is so far from ended that it may be said the executive today has more control over the Commons than Charles I had at any period of his reign."

Prerogative powers enable the Government to exercise powers — to make war, declare peace, ratify treaties, recognise foreign governments, make appointments, for example — without Parliament having any say. They also enable the Government to bypass Parliament by making "Orders in Council", a useful device and a reference to the monarch's Privy Council. The hallmark of the Privy Council is secrecy. When its members are briefed by ministers "on Privy Council terms" it means that they were given "state secrets" that they must not divulge, especially not to ordinary Members of Parliament. The Privy Councillor's oath, drawn up in about 1250, is the earliest weapon in the Government's formidable armoury defending official secrecy. "You will," it states, "keep secret all Matters committed and revealed unto you."

From *The Guardian*, 3 January 1990

Exercise 10   Complete the following sentences.

1 Parliament was stronger before 1688 than now because . . .
2 Prerogative powers mean that Parliament cannot stop the Government . . .
3 The Government can use the Privy Councillor's oath to . . .

Reforms?

Worries over the gradual loss of individual rights under Mrs Thatcher have led the Labour Party to promise to introduce reforms.

Labour reformers to back elected 'Lords'

LABOUR PARTY proposals for a Charter of Rights, safeguarded by an elected second chamber, were set out yesterday by Roy Hattersley, the party's deputy leader.

Dismissing the case for a single, all-embracing Bill of Rights, he argued that a programme of legislation — ranging from a Freedom of Information Act to changes in the criminal justice and employment laws — was a more practical method of guaranteeing and extending civil liberties. A Labour government's reforms would include measures to expose the conduct of the secret services to parliamentary scrutiny.

Although replacement of the House of Lords by an elected second chamber is not a priority for the early years of a Labour Government, Mr Hattersley suggested that such a chamber be given new powers to delay until after a general election any legislation that threatened individual rights. The result would be to protect Labour's changes from a subsequent authoritarian government.

He identified the principal ingredients for a Charter of Rights as:
■ A Freedom of Information Act replacing the law on official secrets with a public "right to know".
■ A Security Services Act bringing the operations of MI5 and MI6 under the general supervision of a Commons Select Committee made up of senior members of Parliament.
■ Reductions in the power of ministerial patronage by giving the Commons a veto over senior appointments such as the chairmanship of nationalised industries, the BBC and various boards. A Commons committee would be entitled to stage American style "confirmation" hearings if a nominee were thought poorly qualified for the job.
■ A Right to Privacy Act "to protect the citizen against intrusion by an increasingly authoritarian state". The Press Council would cease to be funded by newspapers and would have a statutory duty to adjudicate in cases of needless harassment.

Mr Hattersley said the changes would be matched by early commitments to reform the courts and legal system, including an extension of legal aid in order to achieve greater equality before the law. There would be stronger legislation to outlaw discrimination on grounds of race, sex or sexual orientation. The new law would allow closer monitoring of public and private sector recruitment policy and practice.

Employment rights proposed in the European Social Charter would be enacted to provide better protection against unreasonable and arbitrary dismissal. But workplace rights for women could also be enhanced by providing more child care and flexible working arrangements.

Attacking the Government's record on individual rights, the Labour deputy leader accused Mrs Thatcher of an assault on civil liberties.

"No Government in our history has concentrated more power in Whitehall and Westminster", Mr Hattersley declared. "No prime minister in the modern era has been more impatient with dissent, more intolerant of criticism, more determined to bully and bribe broadcasters into providing support."

Paddy Ashdown, leader of the Liberal Democrats, last night attacked the Labour proposals 'as feeble'. He said: "A Bill of Rights is an essential, guaranteed and constitutional buttress for individual freedom, particularly in our centralised and unrepresentative political system."

From the *Correspondent*, 7 January 1990

Exercise 11   Make a list of the proposed reforms.

1 ....

2 *parliamentary scrutiny of the secret services*

3 ....

4 ....

ELECTIONS AND POLITICAL PARTIES

Elections

The right to vote in elections has gradually been extended to virtually every British subject over 18 who is resident in Britain (members of the Royal Family and lunatics are not allowed to vote). People vote for any one of the candidates in the **constituency** in which they are registered. The candidate that obtains the most votes in that constituency, irrespective of whether he or she has an overall majority, becomes its **Member of Parliament** and the other votes are 'wasted'.

Anyone over 21 who is entitled to vote (except for clergymen, civil servants, felons and bankrupts) can stand as a candidate. Candidates are normally selected by the local party associations, but independent candidates can also stand. Each candidate has to pay a deposit (currently £500), which is returned if a candidate obtains at least 5% of the total number of votes cast in that constituency. It is now a tradition for there to be a few humorous candidates in all general elections (such as the 'Don't-Vote-For-Me Party' in the 1987 election).

General elections must be held at least every five years, but the Prime Minister has the right to call elections before the five-year term has expired. Nowadays, the electorate often votes for a particular party leader rather than the party itself, so Government leaders try to hold elections at moments of particular popularity, e.g. Mrs Thatcher after her victory in the Falklands War.

The one-candidate (or **first-past-the-post**) system means that a party can obtain a considerable number of votes nationally but have very few MPs in the Commons, because these votes are distributed evenly among the various constituencies. While not very representative and making it difficult for more than two major parties to co-exist, the system produces stable governments and prevents minority parties from having an undue say in the running of national affairs.

Exercise 12
1. Who can vote in elections in Britain?
2. How many candidates does a person vote for in a general election?
3. What must a candidate do to be elected?
4. Who may stand as a candidate?
5. What does it mean when you 'lose your deposit' in an election?
6. How often are General Elections held?
7. Why can elections in Britain be said to have become 'personalized'?

Exercise 13
Study the two charts below showing the results of the 1987 General Election and explain why the percentage of votes and seats is not the same.

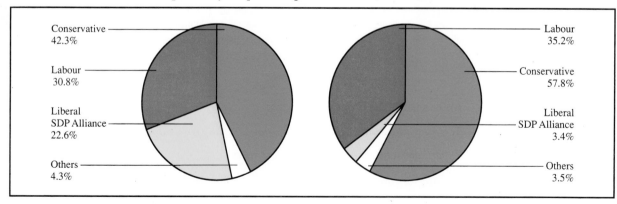

Conservative 42.3%
Labour 30.8%
Liberal SDP Alliance 22.6%
Others 4.3%

Labour 35.2%
Conservative 57.8%
Liberal SDP Alliance 3.4%
Others 3.5%

Political parties

As a result of the electoral system two parties have usually been predominant in Britain, at different times Tories and Whigs, Conservatives and Liberals, and since the 1930s Conservatives and Labour, with one party normally obtaining a majority of seats in the House of Commons and the other having its role limited to criticizing Government policy.

The **Conservative Party** was formed by Robert Peel from what was left of the old Tory party in the 1830s. Peel and his successor Benjamin Disraeli (the first Conservative Prime Minister) together shaped modern Conservatism. Originally the party of church, aristocracy and landed gentry, it has increasingly been supported by large business interests. The **Labour Party** was formed by James Keir Hardie in 1892 to represent the workers and was more or less the parliamentary wing of the Trades Unions, with whom the party continues to be closely associated. James Ramsay MacDonald became the first socialist Prime Minister in 1924.

At present, in addition to the Conservative (Tory) Party and the Labour (Socialist) Party, the recently-formed **Green Party** has begun to threaten the left-of-centre **Liberal Democratic Party** as the nation's 'third' party.

Margaret Thatcher speaking at the 1990 Conservative Party conference

Neil Kinnock at the 1990 Labour Party conference

Paddy Ashdown at the 1990 conference of the Liberal Democrats

Demonstration at the 1990 Green Party Conference

Exercise 14   Complete this table. Find out any information which is not contained in the passage.

Name	Conservative Party	Labour Party	Liberal Democratic Party	Green Party
Also known as	....	....	....	....
Current leader	....	....	....	....
Main support	....	....	....	....

THE JUDICIARY

Parliament, or other bodies acting on its behalf such as local government (and now also the European Community), is responsible for making laws (**statute law**). There is also a large body of laws that have never been codified known as **common law** which has developed from the decisions, based on custom and precedent, taken by judges in court cases.

Criminal law

A person charged by the police with an offence is sent to a **magistrates' court**. Magistrates' courts are presided over by groups of three unpaid, **lay magistrates** (also known as 'justices of the peace' or JPs), who often have no legal qualifications, although they are given basic training when appointed and are advised on points of law and procedure by a legally-qualified clerk. There are also a few **stipendiary magistrates** – full-time, legally-qualified magistrates who sit alone. Magistrates hear and decide in cases concerning minor offences and refer more serious cases to the **Crown Court**. A **defendant** can always choose, however, to be tried by a **jury** in the Crown Court.

The **Crown Court** deals with **trials** of a more serious nature or appeals from magistrates' courts and is presided over by a judge, who must be a **barrister** or a **solicitor** with at least ten years experience. Defendants who declare themselves not guilty of a crime are tried by a **jury** of 12 people. The judge decides on points of law, sums up evidence for the jury and instructs it on the relevant law (as well as determining fines and sentences). It is the jury alone, however, which decides whether a defendant is **guilty** or **not guilty**.

Civil law

Magistrates' courts deal with certain minor questions, while more important matters are dealt with in the **High Court of Justice**, which is both a court of first instance and of appeal. In special cases one of the parties may insist upon trial by jury, which, as well as deciding questions of fact, also fixes the amount of damages to be paid to the injured party. The **House of Lords** is the final court of appeal.

Exercise 15 Complete this flow chart.

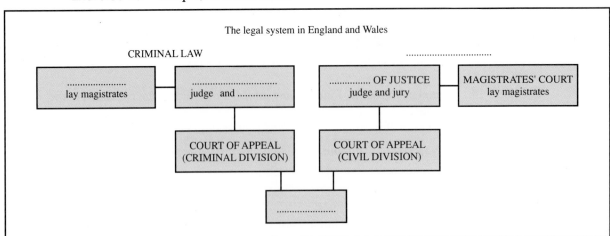

TRADE UNIONS

It was illegal for workers to join together in associations until 1824, but since then these trade unions (so called because they were originally composed of workers practising a given trade) have grown in number and power, and nowadays, despite a sharp decline in membership, almost half the working population belongs to a union. Virtually all the unions are affiliated to the **Trades Union Congress** (**TUC**), which makes it a powerful force in British politics.

Exercise 16 Look at the trade union poster and list the points in favour of trade unions. Then match the following 'problems' as perceived by the Tory governments of the 1980s with the 'solutions' that they adopted.

'Problems'	'Solutions'
'Over-manning' in British industry	Secret ballots before all strikes
Union leaders have too much power ,	No strikes in solidarity with other workers
Sometimes 'against the national interest	No consultation with unions on national affairs
Too many strikes	Removal of negotiating rights from some workers
Too much industry-wide disruption	Abolition of the 'closed shop'

TRADE UNIONS
Working For You

- Better Health and Safety
- Defence Against Unfair Sacking
- Legal Rights
- Representing You at Work
- Representing You on Training Schemes
- Sick Pay and Holidays
- Wage Increases

We're Stronger Together. Join A Union.
TRADE UNION FAIR
The Mall, Central Library, High Road, Wood Green N22.
Friday 20th November 9am – 6pm
Saturday 21st November 9am – 2pm
Special Guest: **Norman Willis, General Secretary TUC.**

Organised by: Haringey Trades Union Council

THE MEDIA

Newspapers

National Newspapers			
Title and foundation date	Circulation average Jan–June 1989	Title and foundation date	Circulation average Jan–June 1989
National dailies		**National Sundays**	
'Populars'		'Populars'	
Daily Express (1900)	1,589,306	*News of the World* (1843)	5,294,317
Daily Mail (1896)	1,750,303	*Sunday Express* (1918)	1,943,089
Daily Mirror (1903)	3,199,103	*Sunday Mirror* (1963)	3,012,143
Daily Star (1978)	912,372	*Sunday Sport* (1986)	530,090
Morning Star (1966)	28,000	*The Mail on Sunday* (1982)	1,961,506
The Sun (1964)	4,173,267	*The People* (1881)	2,660,177
Today (1986)	588,653		
'Qualities'		'Qualities'	
Financial Times (1886)	199,275	*Sunday Telegraph* (1961)	656,120
The Daily Telegraph (1885)	1,113,033	*The Observer* (1791)	693,939
The Guardian (1821)	438,732	*The Sunday Times* (1822)	1,317,865
The Independent (1986)	405,423	*The Sunday Correspondent* (1989)	n/a
The Times (1785)	441,342		

Source: *Audit Bureau of Circulations*

The British are a great nation of readers and, with sales of national newspapers averaging around 15 million copies on weekdays and almost 18 million on Sundays (besides the provincial daily newspapers and the daily evening newspapers that most towns and cities have), only in Japan are more newspapers sold per person than in Britain. The term 'newspaper' can only be loosely applied to the top-selling **dailies**, however, as these **tabloids** contain mainly coverage of 'human' news and scandals, particularly sexual, as opposed to political and economic matters, which are covered in depth in the larger **quality** newspapers. Several of the tabloids even contain pictures of nude girls on page three (Samantha Fox is a famous 'Page Three Girl'). An interesting recent development has been the launching of two 'quality' weekly newspapers – *The Indy* and the *Early Times* – especially for younger readers.

Newspapers in Britain are not subsidized (although the greatest source of income is advertising) and there is no fixed price. They are financially independent of any political party and any political bias results from traditional positions and the influence of the owner. A worrying development has been the concentration of many of the newspapers in the hands of two owners – Rupert Murdoch and Robert Maxwell – especially as a result of the former's evident bias in favour of Mrs Thatcher.

Exercise 17   Complete these sentences to make a summary of the passage.

1 On average, more than one in four people in Britain . . .
2 Newspapers in Britain are classified as either . . .
3 Popular dailies deal with . . .
4 Quality papers cover . . .
5 Recently two newspapers came out intended for . . .
6 The price of newspapers . . .
7 The political position of a newspaper . . .
8 Many people are worried about . . .

Television and radio

Television viewing is by far the most popular leisure pastime in Britain (see pages 4 and 6). The new Broadcasting Bill and the introduction of cable and satellite television are bringing about radical changes in this sector.

Changing TV times

by Vikki Power

IMAGINE turning on the television and finding nothing to watch but game shows and soap operas. Less children's TV, fewer news programmes, no costume dramas or wildlife shows.

Opponents of the Broadcasting Bill, currently going through Parliament on its way to becoming law, say that this is what will happen to British television.

But then imagine even better television than you find now — maybe fewer darts matches and boring documentaries? Supporters of the Broadcasting Bill say that TV and radio will become better because they will contain more of the shows the viewer wants.

Biggest change

The Broadcasting Bill will dramatically change the way British television is operated. The biggest change will be the start up of Channel 5, another TV channel with advertisements, plus three new national radio stations and 200–300 more local ones.

The main intention of the Bill is to make television companies show what people want to watch. **The Independent Broadcasting Authority** (IBA) strictly controls what is shown and when it is shown. The IBA makes sure each ITV company broadcasts a certain amount of news, current affairs programmes and children's TV.

If the Bill becomes law the IBA will be replaced with the **Independent Television Commission** (ITC), a body with a more "hands-off" approach to regulating TV. Some people fear it will be much less strict than the IBA.

Low-quality

Opponents of the Bill are worried that the TV companies will use this freedom to make low-quality programmes like game shows because, compared to **World in Action**, for example, game shows are much cheaper to make and are watched by many more people. If the game show has a larger audience, the TV company can charge more for advertising and make higher profits.

Current affairs programmes (in-depth topical news programmes) have smaller audiences, so they

"The Broadcasting Bill will dramatically change the way British television is operated"

attract fewer advertisers and the TV company makes less money. So critics are worried that ITV companies will cut down on high-quality, expensive programmes.

The Government replies in two ways. First, in order to be able to own an ITV franchise (a franchise gives an ITV company permission to broadcast), ITV companies must promise to show a certain number of 'good quality' programmes. Second, they say that companies will still want to advertise on the less popular shows because they know that a certain type of person watches the show.

Current affairs

For example, Rolls Royce would rather advertise on **World in Action** than on, say, **The Price is Right**. The Government says this will ensure that current affairs and dramas will continue to be made.

The Bill will also affect the BBC by freezing the licence fee from 1991 each television-owning family pays to fund the BBC. The BBC is expected to find other ways of raising money to make programmes, although it will not show commercials.

British television is considered by some to be the best in the world. Whether the Broadcasting Bill will make it better or worse is yet to be seen.

From *Early Times*, 21 December 1989

Exercise 18   List the points made in the article for and against the Broadcasting Bill.

EDUCATION

Schools

Students at a private school in London

One of Britain's comprehensive schools

In Britain it is compulsory for everyone between the ages of 5 and 16 years to receive some officially recognized form of schooling, though most secondary schools continue to provide education until the age of 18. The vast majority of pupils attend **state schools**, which are absolutely free (including all text books and exercise books), but there are also about 500 private schools providing secondary education. The most famous of these schools, confusingly known as **public schools**, are Eton and Harrow.

There is no statutory age at which students change from **primary** to **secondary school**, nor are schools 'specialized' – pupils choose from the numerous subjects taught in their particular school. The recently introduced **National Curriculum** has made it compulsory, however, for three core subjects – English, mathematics and science – and seven other foundation subjects – technology (including design), history, geography, music, art, physical education and a modern foreign language – to be included in the curricula of all pupils. Passage from one academic year to the next is automatic. After a two-year course, usually from 14 to 16 years of age, most pupils take their **General Certificate of Secondary Education** (**GCSE**), assessed on the basis of a mixture of course work and a written examination, in individual subjects. Pupils obtaining at least five passes at GCSE can then specialize for two years (usually from 16 to 18 years of age) in two or three subjects, in which they take the **General Certificate of Education Advanced level** (**A-level**) examination. This is used as an entrance qualification for university (minimum two passes) and other types of higher education, as well as for many forms of professional training.

Exercise 19 Complete this chart.

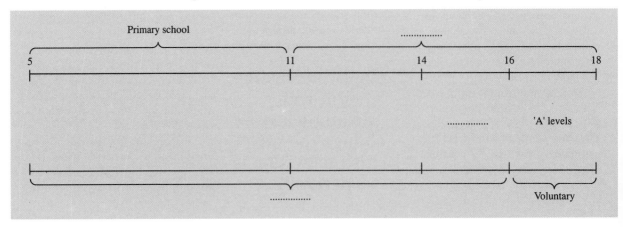

Exercise 20 List and discuss the similarities and differences between schooling in Britain and in your country.

Higher education

Oxford University

Lancashire Polytechnic

There is a considerable choice of post-school education in Britain. In addition to **universities**, there are also **polytechnics** and a series of different types of assisted colleges, such as colleges of technology, art, etc, which tend to provide more work-orientated courses than universities. Some of these courses are part-time, with the students being released by their employers for one day a week or longer periods. Virtually all students on full-time courses receive **grants** or **loans** from the Government which cover their tuition fees and everyday expenses (accommodation, food, books, etc).

Universities in Britain enjoy complete academic freedom, choosing their own staff and deciding which students to admit, what and how to teach, and which degrees to award (first degrees are called **Bachelor** degrees). They are mainly government-funded, except for the totally-independent University of Buckingham.

There is no automatic admission to university, as there are only a limited number of places (around 100,000) available each year. Candidates are accepted on the basis of their A-level results. Virtually all degree courses are full-time and most last three years (medical and veterinary courses last five or six years). Students who obtain their Bachelor degree (**graduates**) can apply to take a further degree course, usually involving a mixture of exam courses and research. There are two different types of **post-graduate** courses – the master's degree (**MA** or **MSc**), which takes one or two years, and the higher degree of Doctor of Philosophy (**PhD**), which takes two or three years.

Exercise 21 Use these notes to make a summary of the text.

1 wide variety – higher education
2 universities – more academic – colleges and polytechnics
3 government grant – fees and maintenance
4 universities independent – financed government
5 entrance – depend 'A-levels'
6 degree – 3 years
7 postgraduate – either . . . or . . .

Exercise 22 Founded in 1969 in Milton Keynes, Buckinghamshire, the **Open University** – so called because it is open to all – does not require any formal academic qualifications to study for a degree, and many 'mature students' enrol. The university is non-residential and courses are mainly taught by post and by programmes on state radio and television. There are, however, short summer courses and special part-time study centres where the students can meet their tutors when they have problems.

List the three or four main differences between the Open University and ordinary universities.

RELIGION

The various Christian denominations in Britain are the result of the various schisms (beginning with Henry VIII) that divided the Church. It is possible to make a very general distinction on a geographical basis between England, which is **Anglican**; Scotland, which is **Presbyterian**; Wales, which is **Calvinistic Methodist**; and Northern Ireland, which is **Protestant**. Obviously, there are large minority groups adhering to other Christian groups in each country. There are also large **Jewish** communities, while immigrants from India, Pakistan and the Middle East have also introduced **Eastern religions**. Indeed, it is now estimated that there are more practising **Muslims** than members of any Christian faith in Britain.

What the survey shows

Which, if any, of the following do you believe in?

		June 1968	June 1975	Mar 1979	Apr 1981	July 1986	Today
The Devil	Yes	21	20	22	21	21	26
	No	60	72	68	73	74	65
	Don't know	19	8	10	7	5	9
Hell	Yes	23	20	22	21	21	24
	No	58	71	66	72	73	65
	Don't know	19	9	12	7	6	11
Heaven	Yes	54	49	57	53	52	55
	No	27	36	31	37	42	34
	Don't know	19	14	12	10	6	11
God	Yes	77	72	76	73	68	64
	No	11	17	15	19	26	24
	Don't know	12	11	9	8	6	12
Reincarnation	Yes	18	28	28	28	25	27
	No	52	58	51	57	62	56
	Don't know	30	20	11	15	13	17

Which of these statements comes closest to your beliefs?

	Feb 1957	Mar 1963	Mar 1979	Apr 1981	July 1986	Today
There is a personal God	41	38	35	36	31	30
There is some sort of spirit or life force	37	33	41	37	41	39
I don't know what to think	16	20	14	15	11	19
I don't think there is any sort of spirit or life force	6	9	8	12	16	12

Do you believe that Jesus Christ was the son of God or just a man?

	Feb 1957	Mar 1963	Mar 1979	Apr 1981	July 1986	Today
Son of God	71	60	55	52	48	46
Just a man	9	16	25	31	32	30
Just a story	6	7	7	5	8	9
Don't know	14	17	13	11	11	15

Which of these comes nearest to expressing your views about the Old Testament?

	Jan 1960	Mar 1979	Apr 1981	July 1986	Today
It is of divine authority and its commands should be followed without question	19	12	14	10	9
It is mostly of divine authority but some of it needs interpretation	41	39	34	38	34
It is mostly a collection of stories and fables	22	33	42	45	43
Don't know	18	16	10	8	14

Which of these comes nearest to expressing your views about the New Testament?

	Jan 1960	Mar 1979	Apr 1981	July 1986	Today
It is of divine authority and its commands should be followed without question	25	13	14	13	10
It is mostly of divine authority but some of it needs interpretation	43	42	39	39	37
It is mostly a collection of stories and fables	13	28	34	39	38
Don't know	19	17	14	9	15

Thinking about the Gospel miracles, do you believe that they are mostly historical facts, mostly the Gospel writers' interpretation of certain events or mostly legends?

	Oct 1984	Today
Historical facts	25	15
Gospel writers' interpretation	38	42
Legends	26	28
Don't know	10	14

Do you think that the Church should or should not take sides in political issues?

	Oct 1984	Today
Should	25	25
Should not	69	67
Don't know	6	8

At the present time, do you think religion as a whole is increasing its influence on British life or losing its influence?

	Feb 1957	May 1967	June 1975	Today
Increasing	17	9	12	12
Losing	52	65	70	69
No change	18	19	12	14
Don't know	13	7	6	6

From *The Sunday Telegraph*, December 1989

Exercise 23 Answer these questions.

1 Does the survey show any change in people's attitude to the Church?
2 Do Britons want an atheist society?
3 What is the attitude of British people towards the Church's involvement in politics?
4 Who are generally the most religious people in British society now?

FINANCIAL INSTITUTIONS

Lloyds of London

Lloyds is not an insurance company, but an organization, almost a kind of club, with more than 8000 separate dealers in insurance called underwriters. Underwriters have no connection with the commercial insurance companies. They do not deal directly with the public, but only through one of the 300 brokers approved by the council of Lloyds. These brokers themselves have no connection with those who handle ordinary insurance business with the public. Lloyds impose very strict rules of professional conduct on their members, and in the rare event of one disobeying, he is expelled.

FLOOR OF LLOYDS WITH UNDERWRITERS

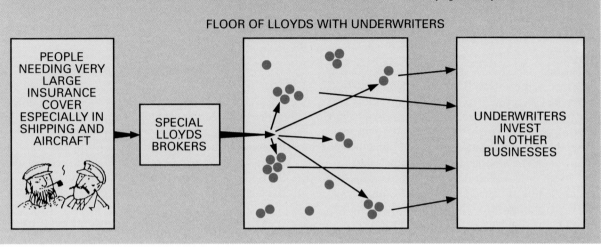

From *Commerce in Action*, OUP

Exercise 24 Use the diagram to describe what someone requiring very large insurance cover must do.

The Stock Market

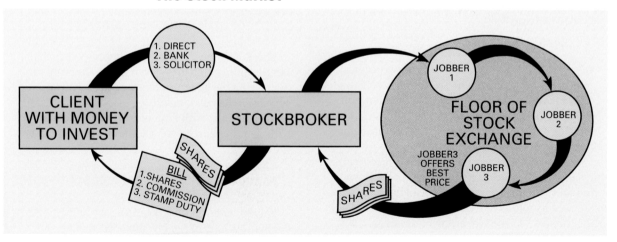

From *Commerce in Action*, OUP

Exercise 25 Use the diagram and the following notes to describe the buying and selling of shares.

1 client approaches broker directly or . . .
2 ordinary people not allowed to deal
3 broker goes to floor of Stock Exchange and . . .
4 jobbers make profit by charging higher price . . .

The Bank of England

Read these extracts from a booklet published by the Bank of England.

The Bank of England is Britain's central bank. It looks after the nation's money, and its work has a direct influence on many aspects of everyday life. Since 1946 the Bank has been publicly owned.

1694 — The beginning

The first step towards central banking was taken with the creation of the Bank of England in 1694, when the Government of the day needed money to pay for the war against France. William Paterson, a Scottish merchant, suggested founding a bank which could then lend its capital to the Government. In the spring of 1694, Parliament gave its approval to an Act which provided for the setting up of a company under the title of "The Governor and Company of the Bank of England". The public were invited to invest in the company and £1,200,000 was very quickly subscribed to what became known as Bank of England Stock.

The Bank was granted a Royal Charter on 27 July 1694 and Sir John Houblon was appointed the first Governor. It opened its books for business in the Mercers' Hall, Cheapside, with a staff of 19. The first notes to bear the name of the Bank of England appeared within a few months of its foundation.

The Bank moved to its present site in Threadneedle Street in 1734.

Banker to the nation

Probably the best known function of the Bank of England is to design, print and issue banknotes in England and Wales, and to store gold in its vaults on behalf of its customers. It does however, have many other responsibilities and functions.

Many of these arose from the Bank's historical development rather than by design. As the Bank gradually withdrew from commercial banking, it extended its role as banker to other banks and to the Government. As the Government's banker, the Bank now acts for the Treasury in raising finances and managing the government debt.

Monetary policy

Monetary policy is directed by the Bank and the Treasury within the policy framework agreed with the Government. The bank cannot act independently of Government, but it plays an important role as adviser on policy and is closely involved in key decisions. Monetary policy operates in the UK mainly through short-term interest rates which are influenced through the Bank of England's daily operations in the money markets.

Foreign exchange

Foreign exchange market intervention is the other principal instrument of monetary policy which has become more prominent since sterling joined the Exchange Rate Mechanism of the European Monetary System in October 1990. Management of the foreign exchange reserves is carried out by the Bank as agent of the Treasury.

Maintaining a sound financial system

One of the Bank of England's most important tasks in maintaining a sound financial system is the supervision of banks operating in the UK, in order to protect depositors. This became a statutory responsibility in 1979 and the powers then granted were strengthened by the Banking Act 1987, which now governs banking supervision.

Helping companies

The Bank's position in the City goes wider than its relationship with banks. It has a responsibility for overseeing the general welfare of the financial services industry. It has also, periodically, acted to help companies with liquidity difficulties to meet with their bankers to see whether a solution can be found.

Promoting efficiency and competitiveness

Finally, in promoting the efficiency and competitiveness of the UK financial system, the Bank endeavours to ensure that payment and settlement systems and other parts of the market infrastructure are sound. The Bank works to remove impediments to the efficient functioning of markets, so that the City can serve industry at home and maintain its place as the world's leading financial centre.

The American people

FACTS AND FIGURES ABOUT THE AMERICANS

How the family was made up

1980

One parent (mother/child)

Two parent 78.5%

18.4%

23.7%

72.7%

One parent (father/child)
3.1%   3.6%   1988

Source: Commerce Department, Census Bureau   By Bob Laird, USA TODAY

Copyright 1989, USA TODAY.
Reprinted with permission.

WHERE THE MONEY WENT ...
U.S. personal consumption
expenditure (billions of dollars)

	1980		1988	
Total	1,732	100%	3,235	100%
Health	187	10.8%	443	13.7%
Travel	238	13.7%	406	12.5%
Food	370	21.3%	597	18.4%
Housing	261	15.1%	501	15.5%
Clothing	135	7.8%	234	7.2%
Recreational goods	115	6.6%	247	7.6%
Other	481	24.9%	807	24.9%

Source: U.S. Bureau of Economic Analysis

Going to the cats

Dogs are still the USA's No. 1 pet, but cats are gaining as dog ownership declines. Percentage of households owning at least one dog or cat:

40.5   37.7   36.2
27.0   28.0   30.0
1982   1985   1989

Source: Pet Food Institute   By Keith Carter, USA TODAY

Copyright 1990, USA TODAY.
Reprinted with permission.

Exercise 1   Study the three charts and describe the changes that occurred in the 1980s with regard to the composition of families, family expenditure, and pet ownership.

LEISURE AND SPORT IN THE USA

The three most popular spectator sports in the USA are American football, baseball, and basketball. But what about participation sports?

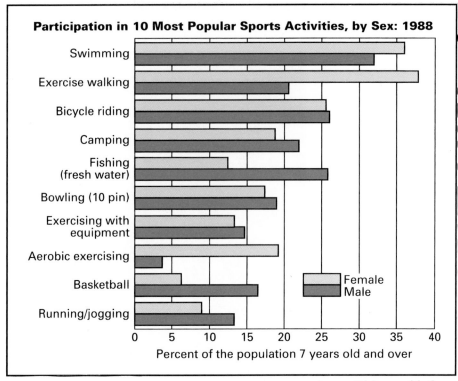

Participation in 10 Most Popular Sports Activities, by Sex: 1988

Percent of the population 7 years old and over

Source: *US Bureau of the Census*

Exercise 2

1 Which is the most popular participation sports activity for men, and which for women?
2 Which activity has exactly the same popularity with both men and women?
3 Which activity is very popular with women, but not very popular with men?
4 Which activity is very popular with men, but not very popular with women?

Exercise 3

Prepare a bar chart like the one above on participation in the ten most popular sports activities in your country. If possible, differentiate the statistics by sex.

If you cannot find official statistics, devise a list of ten sporting activities yourself and conduct a survey of your friends and acquaintances (choosing an equal number of men and women) to see how many of them participate. Express the results in percentages, as in the chart above.

Compare your chart with the American statistics. What similarities are there? What differences?

The American people

YOUNG PEOPLE IN THE USA

College students

College kids 'conservative' about drugs

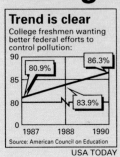

Trend is clear
College freshmen wanting better federal efforts to control pollution:

90
86.3%
80.9%
85
80
83.9%
0
1987   1988   1990
Source: American Council on Education
USA TODAY

By Michelle Healy
USA TODAY

College freshmen are growing more liberal on abortion but more conservative on issues involving drugs and crime, says a survey out today.

The 24th annual survey of college freshmen, by the University of California-Los Angeles and the American Council on Education, also finds the environment was students'

top concern. Survey highlights:

▶ Support for legalized abortion increased sharply from 1988 to 1989 – from 57 percent to 64.7 percent, after holding fairly stable (53 to 59 percent in favor) since 1977.

▶ The share of students favoring legalization of marijuana (16.7 percent) and abolishing the death penalty (21.3 percent) continues to decline; the percentage favoring employer's right to require drug-testing grows

(77.8 percent).

"When it comes to matters of crime and drugs, they're more conservative than they've ever been," says UCLA's Alexander W. Astin, survey director.

▶ 86 percent think the government isn't doing enough to control pollution; 26.1 percent say involvement in environmental cleanup is a "very important" life goal.

▶ A record 36.7 percent joined organized protests in the year before college; 6.3

percent say there's a "very good chance" they'll join college protests, up from 5.4 percent in '88, 4.7 percent in '87.

"The right issue might galvanize some of this energy," says Astin.

▶ 78.2 percent back greater government hand-gun-controls efforts – a new question.

The nationally representative survey drew 216,362 responses from 403 colleges.

Exercise 4 Complete this table about the opinions of 1st-year US college students.

Top concern	More conservative about ....
New concern	More liberal about ....

Pop music

Freedom of speech is considered so basic to American society that it is enshrined in the US Constitution (see page 85). But, as the following article shows, freedom of speech does not always apply to pop songs!

COVER STORY
Free-speech fight strikes new chords

By Jefferson Graham
USA TODAY

In 1956, Frank Sinatra lashed out at a new form of music called rock 'n' roll. It was, he said, an "ugly, degenerate" form of expression that used "sly, lewd, dirty lyrics."

Now, 34 years later, youth music is still under fire. This time it's rap and heavy metal.

"Teen crime, pregnancy, suicide, bizarre and violent behavior – it is

all reflected in a lot of the current music," says Florida state Rep. Joe Arnall, 43, a Republican. "We're talking about songs that go far beyond *Louie, Louie*. It's time for society to say there are certain things we cannot accept."

Last week, a Sarasota, Fla., record store employee was arrested on a felony charge for selling the latest album from rap group the 2 Live Crew to an 11-year-old. A

judge called it obscene and banned its sale in Broward County.

Consumers in Florida may soon find such sales controlled statewide. Lawmakers there and in 11 other states – many of whom grew up on Buddy Holly, Elvis Presley and the Big Bopper – are considering legislation that would, in effect, make it illegal for minors to buy certain albums, CDs or cassette tapes.

Today, country singer Emmylou

Harris will testify before Tennessee's state Senate against one such bill.

Each state has its own twist, but there is one common thread: Music deemed "objectionable" would require a large yellow sticker alerting the consumer that it contains mentions of incest, bestality, sadomasochism, sexual activity, murder, violence or illegal use of drugs or alcohol.

Exercise 5 1 What kind of music did Frank Sinatra attack? What kind of music is being attacked today?
2 Which two states are named in the article as considering legislation against 'objectionable' music? How many other states are mentioned?
3 What is Emmylou Harris's opinion?

─── Business ───

Freed from Greed?

The past decade brought growth, avarice and an anything-goes attitude. But the '90s will be a time for the U.S. to fix up, clean up and pay up

BY OTTO FRIEDRICH

...

The good news is that the U.S. gross national product doubled during the 1980s, from $2.7 trillion to $5.3 trillion. The bad news is that much of this was done by borrowing. The U.S. national debt tripled, from $909 billion to almost $2.9 trillion (interest alone now amounts to $165 billion a year, roughly the equivalent of the budget deficit). Corporate and personal debts both soared. All in all, the U.S. consumed $1 trillion more than it produced in goods and services.

The good news is that lots of people prospered. This was the age of financial wizards making fortunes in their 20s, and roughly 100,000 Americans became millionaires every year. Michael Milken, the junk-bond king at Drexel Burnham Lambert, set the record by earning $550 million in 1987. The bad news is that while the top 20% of American families' earnings rose more than $9,000 (after adjustment for inflation), to

— Michael Douglas as Gordon Gekko in the film *Wall Street*

"Greed ... is good. Greed is right. Greed clarifies, cuts through and captures the essence of the evolutionary spirit ... Greed — mark my words — will save ... the U.S.A."

an average of nearly $85,000, the bottom 20% dropped by $576, to a hungry $8,880. The Government estimates that 32 million Americans — 12.8% of the population — live in poverty, compared with 11.4% a decade ago. And Michael Milken has been indicted on 98 counts of fraud and other misdeeds.

...

The good news is that 20 million new American jobs were created during the 1980s. The bad news is that these new jobs did not come in the FORTUNE 500 companies, which actually cut their work forces by 3.5 million; many of the new 1980s jobs were low-paying service positions.

The good news is that booming international trade is spreading wealth around the world. The bad news is that the U.S. was the world's largest creditor in 1980 but went into the red in 1985, and has become the world's largest debtor. Its trade deficit runs about $150 billion a year. Foreign holdings in the U.S. now amount to $1.5 trillion, compared with $1.2 trillion in U.S. assets abroad. And meanwhile, the grinding poverty of the Third World, by now $1 trillion in debt, has not improved at all. ...

Exercise 6 List all the positive and negative changes that occurred, according to the article, in the US economy in the 1980s.

Positive changes	Negative changes

American geography

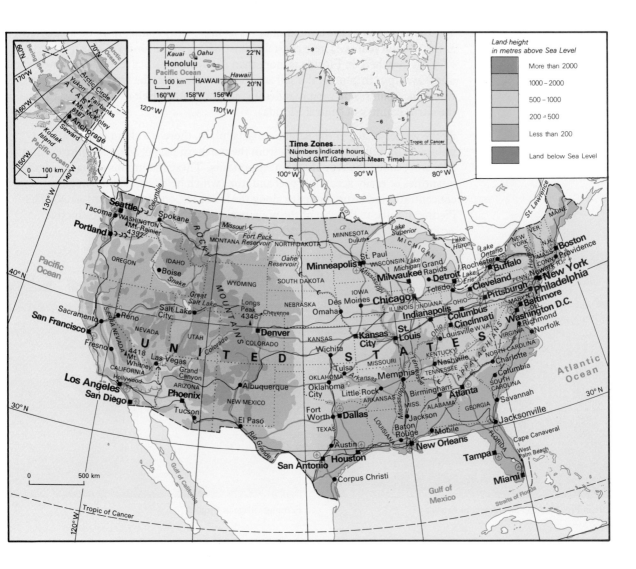

The United States of America is a federal republic of 50 states. There are 48 **conterminous states** which extend from latitude 25°N to 50°N and longitude 125°W to 67°W (4,500 km and four time zones from the Atlantic coast to the Pacific coast); the other two states, Hawaii and Alaska, are situated respectively in the tropical part of the Pacific Ocean (160°W, 3,200 km from the mainland) and near the Arctic circle. The 50 states form an **area** of 3,615,122 square miles (31 times the size of Italy), making the United States the fourth largest country in the world.

Exercise 1

1 Which states do not have a common border with at least one other state?
2 When it is 6 p.m. in Britain, what time is it in . . .

● New York? ● Nashville? ● Denver? ● Los Angeles? ● Anchorage?

PHYSICAL GEOGRAPHY

The country naturally presents a tremendous **variety** in physical features (and climate), ranging from moist rain forest to arid desert and bald mountain peaks. Mount McKinley in Alaska at 20,320 feet (6,194 metres) is the highest point in the United States, while part of Death Valley in California is 282 feet (89 metres) *below* sea level.

The eastern coast of the United States is a long, gently rolling lowland area known as **the coastal plains**. These coastal plains, which stretch from Maine to Texas, are very flat (nowhere in Florida is more than 350 feet above sea level, for example) and often swampy. In general the soil is very poor, except in the fertile southern part, where the plain reaches many miles inland (the **Cotton Belt** of the Old South and the citrus country of central Florida).

At the western edge of the Atlantic coastal plain, there is a chain of low, almost unbroken mountains, stretching from the northern part of Maine southwest into Alabama, called **the Appalachian Mountains**. These mountains contain enormous quantities of easily accessible coal and iron (which helps explain the huge concentration of heavy industry along the lower region of the Great Lakes). The Piedmont hills, to the east of the main peaks, are the most highly productive agricultural land in the country after the Midwest.

Organ Pipe National Monument in Arizona

Farming village in Virginia

The heart of the United States is a vast plain, broken by the Superior Upland and Black Hills in the north and the Ozark Plateau in the south, which extends from central Canada southwards to Mexico and from the Appalachian Mountains westwards to the Cordillera. These **interior plains**, which rise gradually like a saucer to higher land on all sides, are divided into two major parts: the wetter, eastern portion is called the **Central Plains** and the western portion the **Great Plains**, both of which have good soil.

To the west of the Great Plains is the **Cordillera**, which accounts for one-third of the United States. It is a region of tremendous variety, which can be sub-divided into various other regions. On its eastern border **the Rocky Mountains**, a high, discontinuous chain of mountains stretching from mountainous Alaska down to Mexico, rise sharply from the Great Plains. These rugged mountains contain many important metals such as lead, uranium and gold.

The western edge of the Cordillera is characterized by a coastal chain of high mountains, among which there are broad, fertile valleys. The most important ranges are the **Sierra Nevada** and the **Cascades** in the eastern part and the **Coastal Ranges** along the western coast. There is no Pacific coastal plain and between these two sets of mountains there is a large plateau region, with steep cliffs and canyons, basins and isolated ranges. Many basins are rich in resources such as oil and natural gas.

Hawaii is a chain of twenty islands, only seven of which are inhabited. The mountainous islands were formed by volcanic activity and there are still a number of active volcanoes.

Exercise 2   Describe briefly:

- the Coastal Plains
- the Rockies
- the Appalachian Mountains
- the interior plains

The River Mississippi in Iowa

The United States has several immensely long rivers. There are a large number of rivers in the eastern part of the nation, the longest of which is the **Missouri** (3,942 km), a tributary of the **Mississippi** (3,760 km); the Mississippi-Missouri-Red Rock system extends for 6,176 km before entering the Gulf of Mexico near New Orleans. Two other tributaries of the Mississippi – the **Ohio** and **Tennessee** – are more than 1,250 km long. In the West the **Rio Grande**, which forms part of the United States-Mexico border, flows for 3,016 km and only the **Colorado** (2,320 km), **Columbia** (2,240 km) and the **San Joaquim-Sacramento** river systems reach the Pacific.

Exercise 3   Complete this table.

Highest mountain	....
Lowest point	....
Flattest areas	....
Longest river	....
Most northerly state	....
Most westerly state	....

HUMAN GEOGRAPHY

Population

With more than 245,000,000 inhabitants the United States is the fourth country in the world in terms of population. About 75% of the population live in urban areas and there are 170 cities of more than 100,000 inhabitants, 24 of which have populations of over 500,000. Most of these urban centres lie along the Atlantic and Pacific coasts, the Gulf of Mexico and the Great Lakes. The most populous area is the relatively small Northeast, which accounts for nearly one fourth of the nation's population.

In 1990 the US Bureau of Census conducted a new census of the American people which showed that some important demographic changes were taking place.

Census awakens new power cities

Re-ranking cities

1990 Census		1980 Census
1.	New York City	(1)
2.	Los Angeles	(3)
3.	Chicago	(2)
4.	Houston	(5)
5.	Philadelphia	(4)
6.	San Diego	(8)
7.	Dallas	(7)
8.	Phoenix	(9)
9.	Detroit	(6)
10.	San Antonio	(11)

Source: Census Bureau

USA TODAY

By William Dunn
USA TODAY

The once-sleeping giants of the South and West are the new power cities of the 1990s, preliminary Census figures show.

San Diego; San Jose, Calif.; and Jacksonville, Fla., all grew by more than 20% since 1980 — and San Antonio by nearly that much.

The 1990 figures released Wednesday confirm the shift of the USA's power and money away from the North and East.

And they underscore the importance of Sun Belt cities seldom heard from 20 years ago, handing them more federal dollars, a larger voice in Washington and — even more than before — the power to sway presidential elections.

The 1990 Census counted 245,837,683 people in the USA, but is still considered preliminary. Many cities and states will appeal the numbers.

New York is one.

"Do you ... honestly believe that everybody who should be counted has been counted?" asked Gov. Mario Cuomo, referring to his state's smaller-than-expected growth.

But the trend is clear.

▸ New York City remained the nation's largest — about 7 million — but the Census said it lost almost 40,000 residents.

▸ Among the USA's next biggest — Los Angeles, Chicago, Houston and Philadelphia — only the Sun Belt cities grew.

▸ The USA's fastest growing city in the top 50 was Fresno, Calif., a farm town turned high tech. It grew by 61% and has more than 350,000 residents.

Exercise 4

1 Which is the most densely populated area of the United States?
2 What important demographic changes are occurring?
3 Which is the largest city in the United States?
4 Which was the fastest growing city in the 1990 census?

Ethnic groups

The vast majority of the population was **WASP** (White Anglo-Saxon Protestant) until about 1860. Between 1860 and 1920 almost 30 million immigrants arrived from central and southeastern Europe in particular. These mainly Italian, Russian, Polish and Hungarian immigrants quickly formed their own culturally homogeneous neighbourhoods ('Little Italys', etc) and became a second economic class behind the WASPs. The almost 12% of the population that are black are bottom of the economic and educational table, with far higher unemployment than whites, especially as a result of racial discrimination. The most rapidly growing ethnic group is the Hispanics (almost 7% of Americans), who still continue to use Spanish in their homes even though the vast majority were born in the United States. Like the blacks, they have a generally lower economic and educational level than the rest of the population. There are also almost 2 million generally prosperous Oriental Americans (predominantly from Japan, China and the Philippines), who are concentrated mainly in California. The 1.5 million Native Americans live mainly in reserves in the southwestern states in usually deep poverty and there has been little or no integration into American society.

Exercise 5   Complete the pie chart with the missing information. Then give a brief description of immigration to the United States using the information in the pie chart and the flowchart.

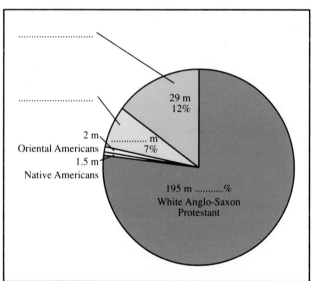

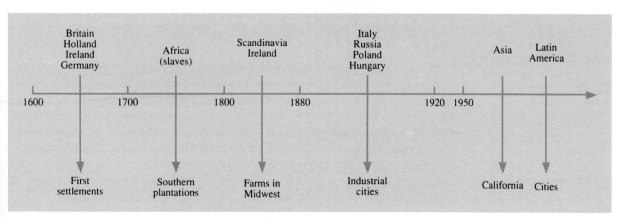

WEATHER AND CLIMATE

Virtually every type of climate can be found somewhere in the United States – from arctic in Alaska to subtropical in Florida. The climate is not generally temperate, despite the latitude, as the tremendous size of the North American landmass heightens the extreme variations in temperature and precipitation, especially in the central regions (in Dakota temperatures have reached a maximum of 49°C and a minimum of −60°C).

Most of the country has a **humid continental climate** with hot summers and cold winters, while the lack of natural barriers either to the north or the south allows cold, dry air to flow south from Canada and warm, humid air north from the Gulf of Mexico, giving rise to spectacular weather of every possible type in the Great Plains and Midwest. Summers are hot and very humid in this region and rainfall decreases to the west as a result of the rain shadow created by the West Pacific range and the Sierra Nevada. The southwest portion of the Great Plains is the hottest and most arid region of the United States, with precipitation, mostly in the form of summer showers, averaging less than 250mm a year.

The Pacific coast is almost rainless in the summer, although there is often fog. In the winter there is frequent drizzle, but the climate remains generally warm and dry, especially in California. The eastern part of the country is moderately rainy, with the precipitation fairly well distributed throughout the year. Summers tend to be extremely humid, specially along the coast of Texas and Florida.

Exercise 6   Complete this table

Weather features	Causes
Climate not generally temperate	*Size of N. America heightens extremes*
Spectacular weather in Great Plains	....
SW part of Great Plains very arid	....

NATURAL RESOURCES

The United States possesses vast non-fuel natural resources. The major resource is **iron**, three-quarters of which comes from the Lake Superior region of the Great Lakes. Other basic metals and minerals mined on a large scale are **zinc**, **copper**, **silver** and **phosphate rock** (used for fertilizers). This wealth is distributed throughout most of the country, but Texas and the West (especially California) are the most important mineral-producing areas. Mining and quarrying account for only about 2% of GNP.

The United States produces one-quarter of the world's **coal** and one-seventh of its **petroleum**, with sufficient coal reserves to last for hundreds of years. About half of the nation's **electric power** comes from coal-fired power stations, while natural and manufactured **gas** supply more than 33% of the nation's power. The main gas fields are found near the main oil fields in Texas, Louisiana and Alaska. **Nuclear power** is also used in many places, using uranium mined in New Mexico and Wyoming, and produces over 10% of the nation's energy output.

Exercise 7   Complete the pie chart on the next page.

Three Mile Island, Harrisburg, the scene of a near nuclear disaster in 1979

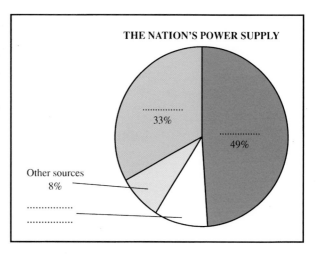

THE NATION'S POWER SUPPLY

.... 33%

.... 49%

Other sources 8%

....

....

TRANSPORT AND COMMUNICATIONS

The vast network of **rivers** and **lakes** in the eastern part of the United States have been of great importance to the economic development of the nation. The Mississippi and its tributaries are all easily navigable and the five Great Lakes, four of which are shared with Canada, are linked to this system by a series of canals. These waterways, together with pipelines and railways, are important for the transport of bulk freight.

By the late 1860s it was already possible to travel from the Atlantic Coast to the Pacific Coast by rail and there is now a vast **railway network** extending over almost the entire country. Railway transport has been largely replaced by **air transport** for long-distance passenger travel, as there is a highly developed network of airline services connecting most towns of importance (and it costs less to travel by air than by train even on comparatively short journeys). Railways are still important for the carriage of certain types of freight, however.

Cars and **trucks** are the most important means of transport for both passengers and goods, and an interstate highway system has been built which provides a route to nearly every major city. On many of these roads a toll has to be paid and the top speed limit anywhere is 55 mph.

Exercise 8 Complete these sentences to obtain a summary of transport systems in the US.

1 The majority of passengers and goods are transported by . . .
2 The most important form of long-distance passenger transport is . . .
3 Railway transport is used for . . .
4 Water traffic is particularly important in . . .

NATIONAL PRODUCTION

The United States is the world's greatest economic power in terms of both Gross National Product and per capita GNP, with its exports accounting for more than 10% of all world trade.

Industry

Although the importance of industrial production is falling and that of services growing (as in most of Western Europe), the United States remains the world's greatest maker of industrial goods and around 20 million Americans are still employed in **manufacturing**. The industrial heart of the nation is the Midwest around the Great Lakes, especially in the region stretching from southern Michigan through northern Ohio and into the Pittsburgh area of Pennsylvania. Another important industrial region is the Northeast, which is the home of the major **computer manufacturers**. **Service industries** are also very important in this region and New York is the country's **banking** and **insurance** capital. The nation's fastest growing region, however, is the Southeast, where the **chemical industry** and **high-technology industries** are now catching up with the traditional **textile** industry as many firms exploit the warm climate and low labour costs.

Exercise 9 Complete this table.

Main industrial area	....
Computer industry	....
Banking and insurance	....
Fastest growing area	....

The top twenty companies

THE WORLD'S BIGGEST

INDUSTRIAL CORPORATIONS

RANK 1988 '87		COMPANY	HEADQUARTERS	INDUSTRY	SALES $ Millions	PROFITS $ Millions
1	1	GENERAL MOTORS	DETROIT	MOTOR VEHICLES	121,085.4	4,856.3
2	4	FORD MOTOR	MICHIGAN	MOTOR VEHICLES	92,445.6	5,300.2
3	3	EXXON	NEW YORK	PETROLEUM REFINING	79,557.0	5,260.0
4	2	ROYAL DUTCH/SHELL GROUP	LONDON/THE HAGUE	PETROLEUM REFINING	78,381.1	5,238.7
5	5	INTERNATIONAL BUSINESS MACHINES	NEW YORK	COMPUTERS	59,681.0	5,806.0
6	8	TOYOTA MOTOR	TOYOTA CITY (JAPAN)	MOTOR VEHICLES	50,789.9	2,314.6
7	10	GENERAL ELECTRIC	CONNECTICUT	ELECTRONICS	49,414.0	3,386.0
8	6	MOBIL	NEW YORK	PETROLEUM REFINING	48,198.0	2,089.0
9	7	BRITISH PETROLEUM	LONDON	PETROLEUM REFINING	46,174.0	2,155.3
10	9	IRI	ROME	METALS	45,521.5	921.9
11	11	DAIMLER-BENZ	STUTTGART	MOTOR VEHICLES	41,817.9	953.1
12	16	HITACHI	TOKYO	ELECTRONICS	41,330.7	989.0
13	21	CHRYSLER	MICHIGAN	MOTOR VEHICLES	35,472.7	1,050.2
14	18	SIEMENS	MUNICH	ELECTRONICS	34,129.4	757.0
15	17	FIAT	TURIN	MOTOR VEHICLES	34,039.3	2,324.7
16	19	MATSUSHITA ELECTRIC INDUSTRIAL	OSAKA	ELECTRONICS	33,922.5	1,177.2
17	15	VOLKSWAGEN	WOLFSBURG (GER.)	MOTOR VEHICLES	33,696.2	420.1
18	12	TEXACO	NEW YORK	PETROLEUM REFINING	33,544.0	1,304.0
19	14	E.I. DU PONT DE NEMOURS	DELAWARE	CHEMICALS	32,514.0	2,190.0
20	20	UNILEVER	LONDON/ROTTERDAM	FOOD	30,488.2	1,485.6

Exercise 10

1 How many of the world's 20 biggest companies are American?
2 In which two sectors do the majority of the companies in the table operate?
3 In which part of the US are most of the American companies located?

Agriculture and fisheries

Farmland in Kansas

Cotton fields in Texas

47% of the land area of the United States is **farmland**, of which 152 million hectares are harvested **cropland** and 560 million hectares are permanent **pasture land**, yet only 6.2 million people live on the nation's 2,300,000 farms. The Midwest is the most important agricultural region in the United States (though California is the number one state in terms of the value of its agricultural products) and alone produces almost twice as much as the American people can consume; corn and wheat are the main crops, and livestock and dairy farming are also carried out on a large scale. Although the South is still important for traditional crops, such as tobacco, corn and cotton, there is now far greater variety, while Texas is the nation's leading producer of cattle, sheep, cotton and rice. The West is important for cattle and wheat farming in the Great Plains area, and for fruit in the fertile valleys of the states that border the Pacific. Yet agriculture (together with fishing) accounts for less than 3% of GNP.

Exercise 11

Complete this table with reference to farmland in the USA.

Farmland	
152m hectares	....
560m hectares	....
Principal products	
Midwest	....
South	....
West	....
Texas	....

American history

PRE-COLONIAL AMERICA

Read this description of some of the early peoples of Central and North America.

Other complex cultures flourished in other parts of the Americas. These peoples varied enormously, ranging from poor nomadic food gatherers of the interior plains of North America to opulent fishing societies of the Pacific Northwest, from the woodland hunting tribes of what is now the northern United States to the wealthy and powerful peoples of Central America. Together, depending upon population estimates reconstructed in our own times, they constituted somewhere between fifty and one hundred million people, of which about ten million lived in North America. Many areas in the western hemisphere contained denser populations than regions of Western Europe in the age of Christopher Columbus. America was not a vacant wasteland awaiting the arrival of "civilized Europeans".

Consider, for example, the chiefdoms of the Pacific Northwest, which included, among others, such groups as the Tlingits of southern Alaska, the Nootka on Vancouver Island, and the Yurok of northern California. These peoples were blessed with an incredibly rich environment based on the vast stock of fish, especially salmon, and abundant edible plants. The large succulent fish annually make their way upstream to spawn and then return to the sea, and the indigenous peoples learned to make nets and weirs to harvest this crop. The natives of the region also developed techniques to preserve their fish, thus assuring sufficient food in seasons of scarcity. The natural abundance encouraged the formation of a sedentary society even though agriculture remained generally undeveloped.

The towne of Pomeiock and true forme of their howses, couered and enclosed some w'th matts and some w'th barcks of trees. All compassed abowt w'th smale poles stuck thick together in stedd of a wall.

Halfway across the continent, from the Great Lakes to the Atlantic seaboard, lived groups of interrelated cultures. Speaking such languages as Siouan, Algonquian, and Iroquoisan, they formed complicated societies that often differed markedly from one another. Relying upon agriculture, as well as on fishing, hunting, and trapping, the peoples of the Eastern Woodlands built stable villages, some of them with as many as five thousand inhabitants. Living either in birch-covered wigwams or in rectangular longhouses, they usually palisaded their villages with log stockades. They also possessed, in their light birchbark canoes, a reliable means of commerce and communication with other tribes.

From *The Free and the Unfree*, P.N. Carroll and W. Noble, Penguin 1977

Exercise 1 List as many differences and similarities as you can between the peoples of the Pacific Northwest and the peoples of the Eastern Woodlands.

Similarities	Differences

COLONIAL AMERICA

The first English settlers in America came to work for private companies which had been granted trading charters by the English Crown, such as the Virginia Company of London which founded Virginia in 1607. These first colonists consisted mainly of the landless, the unemployed and those in search of religious freedom.

The most famous of these early settlers were the 'Pilgrim Fathers', who set sail on the *Mayflower* in 1620 and landed at Cape Cod in New England. As the following contemporary passage shows, the colonists failed to recognize the existing civilizations of America and instead regarded the natives as 'barbarians'.

Being thus arrived in a good harbor, and brought safe to land, they fell upon their knees and blessed the God of Heaven who had brought them over the vast and furious ocean ... But here I cannot but stay and make a pause, and stand half amazed at this poor people's present condition, and so I think will the reader, too, when he well considers the same. Being thus passed the vast ocean, and a sea of troubles before in their preparation (as may be remembered by that which went before), they had now no friends to welcome them nor inns to entertain or refresh their weatherbeaten bodies; no houses or much less towns to repair to, to seek for succor. It is recorded in Scripture as a mercy to the Apostle and his shipwrecked company, that the barbarians showed them no small kindness in refreshing them, but these savage barbarians, when they met with them (as after will appear) were readier to fill their sides full of arrows than otherwise. And for the season it was winter, and they that know the winters of that country know them to be sharp and violent, and subject to cruel and fierce storms, dangerous to travel to known places, much more to search an unknown coast. Besides, what could they see but a hideous and desolate wilderness, full of wild beasts and wild men — and what multitudes there might be of them they knew not.

From *Of Plymouth Plantation*, William Bradford (1590–1657)

Exercise 2

1 How did the Pilgrim Fathers feel when they arrived in America?
2 What did they immediately miss?
3 Were the Native Americans hospitable?
4 What time of year was it when they arrived?
5 Why were the winters particularly dangerous to the settlers?

AMERICAN INDEPENDENCE

By the end of the 18th century, the whole of the Eastern coast of North America had been colonized, largely by the British. The guiding principle for these colonies was the widely-held **mercantilist** view that they should supply the mother country with raw materials and not compete in manufacturing. When Britain asked the colonists to contribute towards the cost of maintaining the British army through centrally-raised **taxes**, there was serious opposition to this 'taxation without representation' (the British Parliament did not contain any American-elected members).

After the taxes had been repealed, there was relative peace everywhere except Boston, but when Parliament exempted the tea of the nearly bankrupt British East India Company from import duties, numerous merchants throughout the colonies were threatened with bankruptcy, and colonial opinion united against the British. So, when the first cargoes of this tea arrived in Boston harbour, the American **Patriots** boarded the three ships on the night of 16 December 1773 and threw the tea into the sea – the famous **Boston Tea Party**.

The signing of the Declaration of American Independence

Parliament reacted to this 'act of vandalism' by closing Boston harbour. Representatives from every colony except Georgia met in Philadelphia in September 1774 and replied by imposing a trade embargo on Britain. As war became inevitable, the colonists met for a second time in Philadelphia in May 1776 and made George Washington their commander-in-chief. The formal **Declaration of Independence** was made on 4 July 1776, including the famous declaration 'that all men are created equal, that they are endowed by their Creator with certain unalienable rights, that among these are Life, Liberty, and the pursuit of happiness'.

The **American War of Independence** lasted over six years. The French entered the war, providing decisive military and economic assistance, after the American victory in the Battle of Saratoga in October 1777. The fighting ended when Washington, aided by the French army and navy, surrounded the British forces at Yorktown in October 1781. The peace settlement signed two years later recognized the independence, freedom and sovereignty of the thirteen colonies.

Exercise 3

1 What decision by the British Parliament helped the cause of American independence, and how?
2 What was the 'Boston Tea Party'?
3 What did representatives of the American colonies decide to do at their first meeting in Philadelphia?
4 What happened at the second meeting?
5 Why was the Battle of Saratoga the turning-point in the war?

Exercise 4

Put the following events in their correct chronological order.

☐ The Boston Tea Party

☐ The Battle of Yorktown

☐ The Battle of Saratoga

☐ The Declaration of Independence

☐ The colonists' first meeting in Philadelphia

19TH-CENTURY EXPANSION

The American Revolution was achieved by the 'original 13 states' on the eastern seaboard. The Treaty of 1783, which ended the war with Britain, gave another huge area of land, further to the west, to the new country, and over the next fifty years the whole of the American mainland was brought under US control. Some of this land was acquired by treaty, such as Florida; some by purchase, such as 'Louisiana' (the Mid-West) which was sold to the US by Napoleon in 1803; and some by war, such as Texas and California, which were ceded by Mexico in the war of 1845–47.

Having gained control of the continent, the Americans began to expand across it, continually pushing westwards from their original settlements, forming new farmsteads, villages and towns in the wilds – and displacing and dispossessing the Native Americans in the process. By the end of the century this form of continuous colonizing or 'pioneering' had led to the settlement of the entire United States from the east coast to the west.

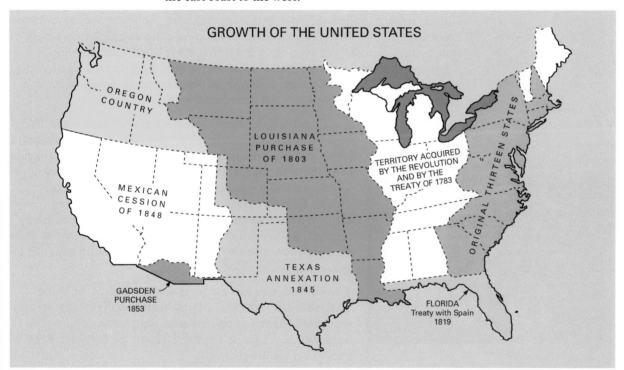

GROWTH OF THE UNITED STATES

Exercise 5   Complete the chronological table with information from the passage and the map.

1783	....
1787	US Constitution signed
1789	George Washington elected first President
1803	....
1819	....
....	Texas annexed to the US
1848	....

THE WAR OF SECESSION (1861–1865)

Expansion brought problems, not least because of the very different societies of the North and the South. The problem of slavery was first raised over the status of Missouri when it was admitted into the Union in 1821.

The anti-slavery movement gained tremendous support after publication of a book called *Uncle Tom's Cabin* by Harriet Beecher Stowe, and political divisions over slavery in the Whig and Democratic parties led to the formation of the **Republican Party**, whose main principle was opposition to the extension of slavery. When the Republican candidate, Abraham Lincoln, was elected President in 1860, South Carolina announced that its Union with all other states was dissolved and was immediately followed by Mississippi, Florida, Alabama, Georgia, Lousiana and Texas, which together formed a **Confederacy** with a constitution based on slavery. The Northerners did not want war and Lincoln in his opening speech as President declared that he would not interfere with slavery in the Southern states, but merely affirmed the constitutional right of the Union to determine the status of new states.

Lincoln refused to allow secession to disrupt the Union, however, and, as civil war became inevitable, Virginia also seceded on the constitutional grounds that every state in the Union enjoyed sovereign rights; Nebraska, North Carolina and Tennessee quickly followed. The twenty-three states of the industrial North, with a population of 22,000,000, were, therefore, opposed by eleven Southern states, almost 4,000,000 of whose 9,000,000 inhabitants were slaves.

The Battle of Gettysburg

The three main theatres of action when war broke out in 1861 were the sea, the Mississippi Valley and the Eastern seaboard states. Although the Union had naval superiority, it was unable to establish an efficient blockade until 1863. In the Mississippi Valley in the West, General Grant and his forces gradually split the Confederacy in two, while in Virginia, Union forces suffered numerous defeats against the two brilliant Southern generals, Robert E. Lee and Thomas 'Stonewall' Jackson. But the South was unable to obtain the decisive victory it needed to gain foreign recognition.

The war became a **lost cause** for the South after the Battle of **Gettysburg** in July 1863, although it heroically fought on until April 1865, when Lee and his army were forced to surrender at Appomattox, Virginia. The war had cost the lives of 618,000 men – over half from disease.

Exercise 6 Complete the following sentences to obtain a brief summary of the American Civil War.

1 The prime cause of the war was . . .
2 The first state to secede from the Union was . . .
3 This was followed by . . .
4 The main theatres of war were . . .
5 The Confederacy inflicted defeats on the North but was unable . . .
6 Victory was achieved by the Union forces at . . .

INDUSTRIALIZATION AND IMMIGRATION

In less than fifty years, between the Civil War and the First World War, the United States was transformed from a rural republic into an urban state. The nation's economic progress, based on iron, steam and electrical power, was speeded up by thousands of inventions like the telephone and typewriter, but the terrible working and living conditions, and the unfair monopolies that characterized the industrial revolution in Britain, were repeated on an even bigger scale.

An important factor was continuous and unrestricted immigration from Europe. While many of the 5 million immigrants who had come over between 1850 and 1870 had been able to obtain cheap land in the west, this was no longer possible for the 20 million people who poured into the country between 1870 and 1910 (mainly from southern and eastern Europe) and who were eager to work at almost any wages and under almost any conditions. The often better-educated blacks, who had left the South in search of work, became the object of violent racial discrimination, particularly on the part of the newly arrived white immigrants, and were forced into ghettoes.

Industrialist Andrew Carnegie

Virtual monopolies were created in every sector through mergers and takeovers and the great captains of industry like Rockefeller in oil and Carnegie in steel, with their enormous economic and political power, were the representative figures of the age. While they enabled the United States to invade Europe with its manufactures and brought the benefits of large-scale production to almost every American home, legislative changes were needed to control the power of these **trusts**. President Teddy Roosevelt, a Republican, began a social crusade in 1901 with the help of the progressive members in both the Democratic and Republican parties. The activities of trusts were regulated and legislative reforms were introduced to improve general living and working conditions (such as an eight-hour working day). Woodrow Wilson, a Democrat, added even more profound reforms. Protective tariffs were substantially reduced, a new anti-trust law was introduced and other important reforms were carried out in the field of agriculture and labour.

Exercise 7   Use these notes to prepare a brief summary of the passage.

50 years – rural republic – urban state
inventions – accelerated – industry
social problems – especially because – immigrants
mass production – goods – every household
captains of industry – too powerful
Roosevelt and Wilson – reforms – regulate trusts

Exercise 8   Use the pie charts to describe the changes in immigration patterns between 1890 and 1910.

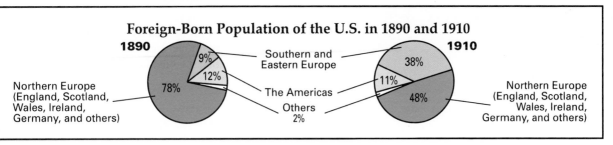

Foreign-Born Population of the U.S. in 1890 and 1910

1890
9%
12%
78%
Southern and Eastern Europe
Northern Europe (England, Scotland, Wales, Ireland, Germany, and others)
The Americas
Others 2%

1910
38%
11%
48%
Northern Europe (England, Scotland, Wales, Ireland, Germany, and others)

AMERICA AND TWO WORLD WARS

World War I

America was determined to stay out of the First World War and adopted a policy of strict neutrality. However, attacks on passenger ships by German submarines and the discovery of a German plot to involve Mexico in war with the United States led Congress to declare war on Germany in April 1917.

The arrival of two million fresh troops altered the balance sufficiently to enable the Allies to win the war. While the Americans were in favour of a non-punitive settlement, Wilson was unable to prevent the Allies from trying to further their imperialist ambitions in the peace settlement and the Republican-controlled Senate refused to ratify the **Treaty of Versailles**, which also contained Wilson's idealistic **League of Nations**. The United States, therefore, never took its leading role in the organization which Wilson had hoped would end wars.

Exercise 9
1 What was America's original policy during World War I?
2 What made Congress change its mind?
3 Why didn't America participate in the League of Nations?

THE ROARING TWENTIES

The Roaring Twenties

The 1920s were a decade of conservatism and insecurely founded prosperity, in which tariffs were brought to their highest ever levels and taxes were drastically reduced. This remarkable rise in living standards, which caused the decade to be called the **Roaring Twenties**, ended suddenly in October 1929 with the Wall Street crash – the result of a long period of over-production by the nation's factories and farms, and speculative mania among the middle and wealthy classes. This crash marked the beginning of the worst depression in American history, commonly referred to as the **Great Depression**.

The period was full of contrasts. There was widespread fear following the Russian Revolution that communists would overthrow the Government (the **Red Scare**), which led to the persecution of all left-wing groups; there was briefly mass support (four million members in 1925) for the Ku Klux Klan, which, in addition to blacks, now attacked Catholics, Jews and all those not born in America; and restrictions were imposed on immigration, not only with regard to the number but also the countries of origin. Morever, this was the period of **prohibition**, when it was prohibited by the Eighteenth Amendment (1919) to manufacture, transport or sell intoxicating liquors (when it ended in 1933, only eight states stayed 'dry').

Unemployed queuing for Sunday dinner during the American Depression

Yet the Twenties were also a period of sexual revolution 'when the existence of an instinctive "sex drive" in young people, especially women, gained social acceptance. . . [and] sexual problems and analysis became acceptable and then fashionable', and of mass culture, when radio and magazines began to present standardized behaviour models to the population with its culturally different backgrounds, and Hollywood fostered the myth and illusion on which the whole decade had been built.

Exercise 10 List the issues and contrasts of the 1920s under two headings.

Positive	Negative

THE NEW DEAL ERA

The construction of Fort Loudon Dam, which gave employment to thousands

Franklin D. Roosevelt blamed the Depression on basic faults in the American economy and promised a 'new deal' for the 'forgotten man'. He won the 1932 presidential election with an unprecedented majority and set about remedying the worsening situation with his **New Deal** in 1933. This was the first administration to introduce government planning into the economy. Over the next two years, millions of unemployed were given jobs in public works projects, and emergency relief was provided for others in order to create greater internal demand for American products. Numerous measures were also taken to help the farmers, as a result of which their incomes more than doubled between 1932 and 1939. The Second New Deal (1935–39) aimed at providing security against unemployment, illness and old age, to prevent the terrible hardships of the Depression being repeated.

Exercise 11 Complete the flowchart with information from the passage.

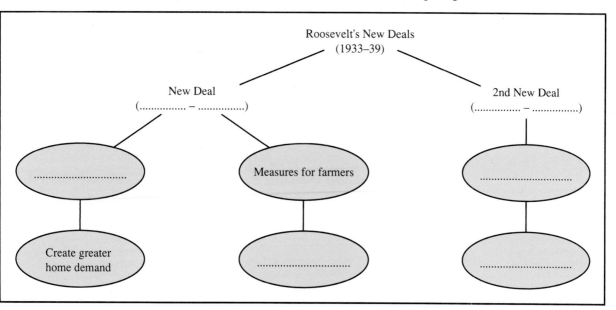

WORLD WAR II

Roosevelt once said in defence of his New Deal that continuing unemployment and insecurity were partially to blame for the disappearance of democracy in Germany, Italy and Spain, where the ordinary people had turned to strong governments for their intervention. This rise of totalitarian governments influenced his foreign policy, which was in opposition to the isolationist basis of Congress's **neutrality acts**. Once war had come to Europe, few Americans were truly neutral. Roosevelt was, therefore, able to provide all possible aid to Great Britain 'short of war' and still become the first President to be elected for a third term.

Churchill, Truman and Stalin at the Potsdam Conference

Relations with Japan continued to worsen and, while negotiations were underway between the two countries, the Japanese attacked the American naval base at Pearl Harbor in Hawaii on the morning of 7 December 1941. Congress responded by immediately declaring war on Japan.

Although Roosevelt and Churchill decided that the main theatre of the war should be Europe, the American navy obtained several victories against the Japanese in 1942 and gradually reconquered one island after another in the Pacific. In Europe the Germans were slowly pushed back on all sides before surrendering on 8 May 1945. While the Japanese position was equally hopeless, they refused to surrender and the prospect of a heavy loss of life convinced the Allies to drop atomic bombs on Hiroshima on 6 August and Nagasaki on 9 August, leading to Emperor Hirohito's formal surrender on 2 September 1945.

The **United Nations Charter** had been drafted at the Potsdam peace conference in July 1945. This ended American isolationism and recognized the nation's important role in international affairs.

Exercise 12   Complete this table with information from the passage.

Event	Date
1 Pearl Harbor	....
2	1942–4
3	6 June 1944
4 Germany surrenders	....
5	July 1945
6	6 August 1945
7 Japan surrenders	....

POST-WAR AMERICA: THE COLD WAR

From Stettin in the Baltic to Trieste in the Adriatic, an iron curtain has descended across the Continent. Behind that line lie all the capitals of the ancient states of central and eastern Europe. Warsaw, Berlin, Prague, Vienna, Budapest, Belgrade, Bucharest and Sofia, all these famous cities and the populations around them lie in what I must call the Soviet sphere, and all are subject, in one form or another, not only to Soviet influence but to a very high, and in many cases, increasing measure of control from Moscow.

from a speech made by Winston Churchill at Westminster College, Fulton, Missouri, on 5 March 1946.

Nobody took Churchill's words more seriously than the Americans. The fear that Greece and Turkey might fall behind this **iron curtain** led Truman to ask Congress for funds to help 'all free peoples' to resist Communist aggression – the **Truman Doctrine**. The widespread fear of Communism was one of the reasons behind the creation of the **North Atlantic Treaty Organization** (**NATO**) in April 1949.

The desire to keep Europe free of Communism was also behind the **Marshall Plan**, devised by US Secretary of State George Marshall in 1947, in which the USA gave or loaned billions of dollars to various European countries, particularly Germany, to assist in post-war reconstruction of their industries.

The persistent hostility between the Western and Communist nations came to be called the **Cold War**, which became a real war in 1950 when Soviet-trained North Korean troops invaded the Republic of Korea. Numerous incidents throughout the world increased international tension and the possibility of another global conflict. This nearly occurred in 1962 when the United States learned that there were Soviet-manned missile bases in **Cuba**. The Russians only removed the missiles after a naval blockade had been established around the island.

There was a widespread fear of Communism in America during the 1950s. The most famous anti-Communist was Senator Joseph McCarthy of Wisconsin. Anyone who dared to oppose him was branded as a Communist or 'Communist sympathizer'. He used his method of discrediting people without proof so often that it became known as **McCarthyism**. Those accused of being pro-Communists usually lost their jobs and found it very difficult to get new ones.

Exercise 13 Give a brief description of:

1 The Cold War
2 The Marshall Plan
3 The Truman Doctrine
4 McCarthyism

CIVIL RIGHTS

The issue that dominated American politics in the 1950s and 1960s was civil rights.

Numerous Presidents attempted to improve the situation of **black people** (and other minorities) in American society. President Truman appointed the first black judge in the Federal court system and some progress was made towards racial integration in schools, restaurants and transportation in the South by Eisenhower, Kennedy and Johnson, despite congressional opposition. The blacks themselves, led by people like the Reverend Martin Luther King, became increasingly active in attempting to improve their status and numerous non-violent protests began in 1960 to speed up the end of segregation. In the mid-1960s these mass demonstrations often degenerated into violent clashes, as the militant Black Power movements replaced the non-violent organizations.

Exercise 14

1 Who opposed the post-war Presidents in their attempts to lessen racial discrimination?
2 What did Martin Luther King want to end?
3 How did the Black Power movement differ from King?

Exercise 15

'I have a dream that my four little children will one day live in a nation where they will not be judged by the colour of their skin but by the content of their character.'

Have Martin Luther King's words, spoken in 1963, come true?

Martin Luther King on a Civil Rights march

Exercise 16 Discussion

What do you know about the position of black people and other minority ethnic groups in America today? In which sectors have black people been most successful? Have Dr King's dreams been realized? Discuss the findings of the 1990 census reproduced below.

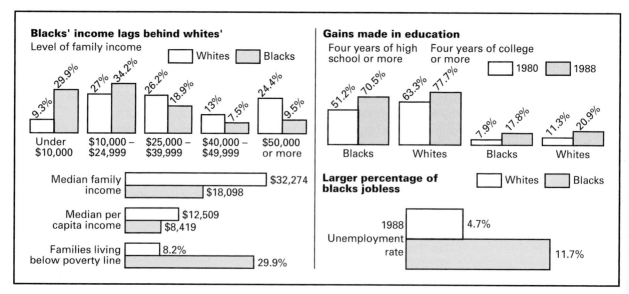

Blacks' income lags behind whites'

Level of family income

Whites / Blacks

	Under $10,000	$10,000 – $24,999	$25,000 – $39,999	$40,000 – $49,999	$50,000 or more
Whites	9.3%	27%	26.2%	13%	24.4%
Blacks	29.9%	34.2%	18.9%	7.5%	9.5%

Median family income — $32,274 / $18,098

Median per capita income — $12,509 / $8,419

Families living below poverty line — 8.2% / 29.9%

Gains made in education

Four years of high school or more / Four years of college or more

1980 / 1988

	Blacks (high school)	Whites (high school)	Blacks (college)	Whites (college)
1980	51.2%	63.3%	7.9%	11.3%
1988	70.5%	77.7%	17.8%	20.9%

Larger percentage of blacks jobless

Whites / Blacks

1988 Unemployment rate: 4.7% / 11.7%

Source: *US Bureau of the Census*

American history

CRISIS: VIETNAM AND WATERGATE

America's radical fear of Communism got the nation involved in war in **Vietnam**, which in 1954 had been divided into South Vietnam and the Communist Republic of North Vietnam. Elections were to have been held after two years to reunite the two Vietnams, but South Vietnam, supported by the United States, refused to hold the elections, fearing that the popular leader of the North, Ho Chi Minh, would win. As guerrilla attacks by the Communist Viet Cong in South Vietnam increased, President Kennedy (1960–63) began to send military equipment and supplies, and military advisors. American involvement escalated under President Johnson with air raids on North Vietnam and by 1967 there were 464,000 American soldiers in Vietnam. As a result of massive demonstrations throughout the United States, President Nixon began to wind down American involvement in a war that was both unpopular and impossible to win. After the withdrawal of American combat troops in 1973, the South Vietnamese troops put up little resistance and by 1975 Vietnam had been united under Communist control.

Exercise 17   Complete the chronological table of events in Vietnam

1954	....
1956	....
1962	....
1967	....
1969–72	....
1973	....
1975	....

President Nixon makes his resignation speech

While Americans were still recovering from the shock of their first-ever defeat in war, their belief in the nation's political institutions was shaken by a series of **scandals**. The most serious of these became known as the **Watergate** scandal, when prominent members of the Republican party were found guilty of 'bugging' the Democratic party's campaign headquarters (at the Watergate building). The scandal involved President Richard Nixon and eventually forced him to resign the Presidency, thus completely over-shadowing his achievements while in office, such as the normalization of relations with China and the signing of the first **Strategic Arms Limitation Treaty** (**SALT**) with the Soviet Union in 1972.

The Americans reacted to these scandals by voting a series of honest and honourable, but often rather unimaginative politicians into office at national, state and local level for the rest of the 1970s. Moreover, Congress refused to collaborate with Presidents Ford and Carter, so little was done to tackle the country's economic problems of high inflation and unemployment.

Exercise 18   1 What was Watergate? Why was it called 'Watergate'?
2 How did the Americans react to the scandal?
3 Why were the country's economic problems not tackled in the 1970s?

RIGHT-WING RECONSTRUCTION

The election of Ronald Reagan and a Republican administration in 1980 led to an attempt to cut back the amount of national government finance available for non-defence spending, especially social programmes. This together with tax cuts proved popular and helped the nation enter a period of non-inflationary growth.

Abroad Reagan replaced the policy of détente (an easing of tense political relations with Communist nations) with a tougher line against the Soviet Union, which he called the 'evil empire'. He also took a hard line against terrorism, which included invading Grenada and carrying out an air-raid on Libya. The success of his approach helped restore American confidence in its role as world leader.

Ex-President Ronald Reagan, standing beneath a portrait of Karl Marx, addresses members of the U.S.S.R. Supreme Soviet

Towards the end of his second term, however, President Reagan adopted a softer line in foreign affairs, at least towards the Soviet Union. Urged on by massive peace movements in the Western world, the two superpowers made significant progress towards nuclear disarmament, a process which was continued by Reagan's successor as President, George Bush.

Exercise 19
1 In which sector did President Reagan cut government spending most of all?
2 In what way was his initial foreign policy different from that of his predecessors?
3 How did his foreign policy change towards the end of his Presidency?

The United States and the Soviet Union last weekend proclaimed the start of a new chapter in East-West relations at the storm-buffeted summit off Malta. **Mike Harvey** reports on the talks

Cold war over - it's official

THE COLD War officially ended last weekend as a new era in superpower relations was ushered in by President Bush and Mikhail Gorbachev at their historic summit meeing off Malta.

It was an extraordinary summit in every respect. What had been planned as a cosy "feet up" chat on board ship became a formal summit of global importance, largely due to last month's events in eastern Europe.

Malta had seemed an ideal spot for a quiet superpower meeting — neutral, sunny and private. But nobody reckoned on the winter storm which churned up the sea so much that the talks had to be held on board a Soviet cruise ship, the *Gorky,* anchored in the safety of the Maltese harbour.

However, there was no question of the weather ruining the summit. On the Saturday, as Mr Bush stood on the deck of the *USS Belknap* afer a night of being tossed around by the 60mph gale, he displayed the true grit of the navy pilot he once was. Was the weather bothering him? "Hell, no, the summit's going just fine, thanks," he told a group of reporters who had managed to reach the ship.

Mr Gorbachev, trying hard not to gloat over the fact that it was only the presence of the Soviet cruiser that saved the day, said: "This whole incident shows that we can adjust to changing circumstances very well."

At the end of the summit the two leaders offered the prospect of sweeping new arms cuts and a chance for the Soviet Union to join the mainstream of the world ecomony. A joint statement said they now believe they can conclude two new arms control agreements next June, one cutting strategic nuclear weapons in half, and another reducing conventional forces in Europe. They also hope to be ready to destroy their chemical weapon stocks.

In the first-ever joint press conference given by the leaders of the United States and the Soviet Union, Mr Gorbachev said the two superpowers were entering a "new epoch". He said the Soviet Union would "never start a hot war against the United States ... and I'm sure the President of the United States would never start a war against us."

While the two leaders discussed changes in eastern Europe, they were careful not to make any statements that could be seen as interfering in the reforms being carried out in those countries. Mr Bush symbolically suggested Berlin as host city for the Olympic Games in 2004.

The American president also proposed the relaxation of trade barriers, opening the way for American businessmen to look more favourably on investment in the Soviet Union.

This first meeting between Mr Gorbachev and Mr Bush since becoming President confirms that the icy rhetoric of the cold war years is a thing of the past. Even the weather could not dampen the obvious goodwill that now exists between the two leaders.

From *The Indy*, 23 November 1989

Exercise 20

1 When did the Cold war officially end, according to the article?

2 What events had made this meeting between Bush and Gorbachev so important?

3 What happened at the end of the summit for the first-ever time?

4 What did Mr Gorbachev promise? What did he ask President Bush to promise?

American institutions

THE CONSTITUTION

The American Constitution is based on the doctrine of the **separation of powers** between the **executive**, **legislative** and **judiciary**. The respective government institutions – **The Presidency, Congress** and **The Courts** – were given limited and specific powers; and a series of **checks and balances**, whereby each branch of government has certain authority over the others, were also included to make sure these powers were not abused. Government power was further limited by means of a dual system of government, in which the **federal government** was only given the powers and responsibilities to deal with problems facing the nation as a whole (foreign affairs, trade, control of the army and navy, etc). The remaining responsibilities and duties of government were reserved to the individual state governments.

Article V allowed for **amendments** to be made to the Constitution (once passed by a two-thirds majority in both houses of **Congress** and then ratified by the **legislatures** of three-fourths of the states). The Constitution finally ratified by all thirteen states in 1791 already contained ten amendments, collectively known as the **Bill of Rights** (the freedoms of religion, speech and the press, etc), to protect the citizen against possible tyranny by the federal government. So far only twenty-six amendments have been made to the Constitution.

Exercise 1   Make notes on the American constitution under these headings:

Based on: ....

Restrictions: ....

Flexibility: ....

Exercise 2   Look at the chart below and say how the President, Congress and the Judiciary check one another.

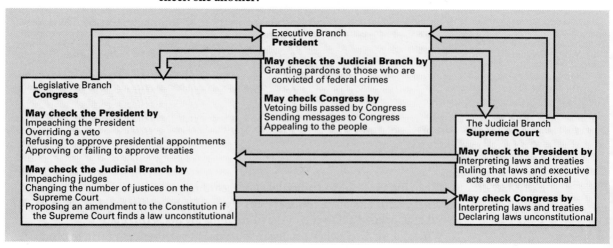

THE PRESIDENCY

The President (any natural-born citizen over 34) is elected for a term of four years and can only be re-elected for one more term (**22nd amendment** – adopted after Franklin D. Roosevelt's four successive terms). The President was originally intended to be little more than a ceremonial Head of State, as well as Commander in Chief of the armed forces, but the federal government's increasing involvement in the nation's economic life and its prominent role in international affairs, where secrecy and speed are often essential, has increased the importance of the Presidency over Congress.

The US Presidential Seal

The President's Oval Office at the White House

The President now proposes a full legislative programme to Congress, although the President, the **Cabinet** and staff are not, and cannot be, members of Congress. This means that the various bills must be introduced into the House of Representatives or Senate by their members. The President is consequently completely powerless when faced by an uncooperative Congress. Given also the difficulties in ensuring that the laws passed are effectively implemented by the federal bureaucracy, it has been said that the President's only real power is the power to persuade.

The role of the Vice-President is not very well defined by the Constitution, which gives him or her no other task than presiding over the debates in the Senate, where he may only vote in the case of a tie. Yet the Vice-President takes over from the President in case of death, resignation, or sickness, which has already happened on eight occasions. To try and attract able men to this otherwise unimportant, mainly ceremonial post, Vice-Presidents have recently been given more important tasks, especially in foreign affairs.

Exercise 3   Make notes on the functions of the President and Vice-President.

	President	Vice-President
Original functions:	....	....
	....	....
Recent functions:	....	....

CONGRESS

The legislative branch of national government consists of two houses – the Senate and the House of Representatives – each with a different role, different powers and a different electoral procedure.

The House of Representatives

The House of Representatives is the dynamic institution of the federal government. The states are represented on a population basis and are divided into **congressional districts** or **constituencies** of roughly equal size (around 520,000 people). There are currently 435 members, who are elected every **two** years. All states must by law adopt the system of single-member constituencies with a simple majority vote. Vacancies arising from death, resignation, etc, are filled by **by-elections**.

The chairman of the House of Representatives, the **Speaker**, is elected by the House and has important responsibilities, giving him considerable influence over the President. Moreover, should the President and Vice-President die before the end of their terms, it is the Speaker who becomes President.

The Senate

The Senate is the conservative counterweight to the more populist House of Representatives. Each state has two senators who, since 1913 (**Seventeenth Amendment**), have been chosen directly by the electorate in the way decided by the state legislature in each state. Senators are elected every **six** years, but the elections are staggered so that one-third of the Senate is elected every two years. A vacancy caused by death or resignation is filled until the next congressional elections by the nomination of the State Governor. There are currently 100 senators. The Senate has the special privilege of **unlimited debate** to safeguard the rights of minorities, but this can enable a small group of Senators to prevent the passage of a bill (**filibustering**).

Exercise 4 List the differences between the House of Representatives and the Senate.

House of Representatives	Senate
dynamic	*conservative*

American institutions

FUNCTIONS OF CONGRESS

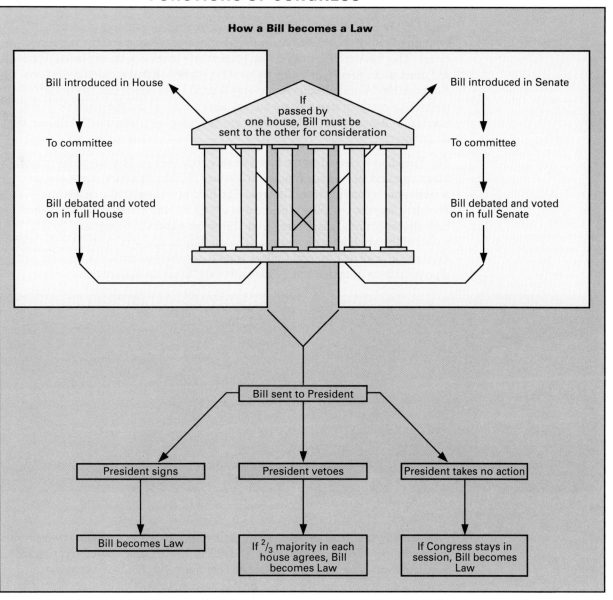

How a Bill becomes a Law

Bill introduced in House
↓
To committee
↓
Bill debated and voted on in full House

If passed by one house, Bill must be sent to the other for consideration

Bill introduced in Senate
↓
To committee
↓
Bill debated and voted on in full Senate

Bill sent to President

President signs → Bill becomes Law

President vetoes → If $^2/_3$ majority in each house agrees, Bill becomes Law

President takes no action → If Congress stays in session, Bill becomes Law

Although Congress can legislate, as shown above, its most important task has become that of scrutinizing the policies and actions of the executive, and upholding the interests of states and districts. Indeed, since Representatives and Senators depend on the voters in their various states or constituencies for re-election, they tend to satisfy the particular interests of constituents and special groups rather than tackle the problems of the nation as a whole. Congress also controls the nation's finances and its permanent specialist staff helps Congress consider and change the budget presented each year by the President.

Exercise 5   List the four functions of Congress as described in the passage.

1 ....   3 ....

2 ....   4 ....

Exercise 6   Look at the chart above and describe how a Bill becomes a Law.

ELECTIONS AND POLITICAL PARTIES

Each US State is free to determine its own electoral laws, subject to certain limitations imposed by the Constitution, national legislation and the Supreme Court. This has enabled many states, particularly in the South, to prevent blacks and other minorities from voting by such means as **poll taxes** and **literacy tests**. After the 1965 Voting Rights Act (giving federal government officials the job of registering voters in states where literacy tests are used) and the abolition of poll taxes (24th Amendment), black voters are now proportionally only 10% fewer than white voters.

The President is elected on the first Tuesday after the first Monday in November of a leap year and takes office at noon on January 20. The President is not elected directly, but by an **Electoral College**. The Electors who actually choose the President are now completely pledged in advance to one person and their names have almost entirely disappeared from the **ballot papers** to be replaced by the names of the candidates themselves. The candidates who win the most votes within a state receive all its Electoral College votes (equal to the number of senators and representatives from that state), no matter how small the majority.

Republican presidential candidate Bush, 1988

Democratic presidential candidate Dukakis, 1988

Presidential candidates are selected by their respective party's national conventions in the summer of each election year. The delegates attending that convention are associated with a particular candidate and are normally chosen either at state conventions of party members (the **caucus** system) or at **state primary elections** held in the preceding months. In a **closed primary** only registered party members can vote, while in an **open primary** any voter can participate (obviously voting in only one party's primary election).

Exercise 7   Answer these questions to obtain a summary of the passage.

1 Who decides who has the right to vote?
2 What is the Electoral College?
3 How do the members of this Electoral College decide how to vote?
4 Who chooses a party's presidential candidate?
5 How are the delegates at the national party conventions chosen?
6 What is the difference between a closed and an open primary?

Exercise 8   Look at the Bush-Dukakis election results and explain why Dukakis received 46% of the votes cast, but only around 20% of the 538 electoral college votes.

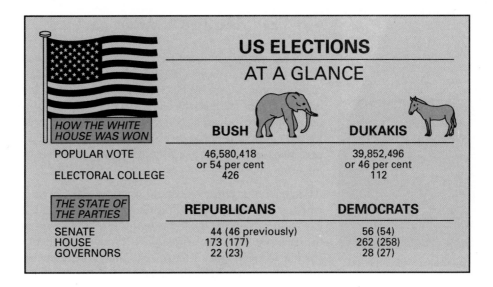

US ELECTIONS AT A GLANCE		
HOW THE WHITE HOUSE WAS WON	BUSH	DUKAKIS
POPULAR VOTE	46,580,418 or 54 per cent	39,852,496 or 46 per cent
ELECTORAL COLLEGE	426	112
THE STATE OF THE PARTIES	REPUBLICANS	DEMOCRATS
SENATE	44 (46 previously)	56 (54)
HOUSE	173 (177)	262 (258)
GOVERNORS	22 (23)	28 (27)

Political parties

Political parties or 'factions' were not mentioned in the original Constitution. Differences over the role of the federal government led to the first national parties – the Federalists and the Republicans. Since then two major parties have dominated political life. The Democratic Party has existed in one form or another since the beginning of the 1800s and has been opposed in successive eras by the Federalist, Whig and Republican parties. The Republican Party was founded in 1854 and was originally the anti-slavery party.

There is very little ideological difference between the Democratic and Republican parties, as both parties defend the free-enterprise capitalist system, accepted by almost all Americans as the basis of American society. The Democrats, unlike the Republicans, tend to favour some Government intervention, but both parties have liberal and conservative wings, and in Congress the liberal and conservative wings of the two parties often side with each other against the other wing. It is broadly possible to say that poor people vote for the Democrats and wealthy people for the Republicans. American politics are the politics of pragmatism and a party will always alter its **platform** to try and catch the mood of the nation, **the middle ground**.

On the same day as the electors vote for the President, they also vote for Senators, members of the House of Representatives, state governors and a host of minor officials. It was once common for people to vote **the straight ticket**, whereby a single cross against the party label on the ballot paper means a vote for every one of the party's candidates from the President downwards, but this is now rare. This explains why there have been a succession of Republican Presidents and Democrat majorities in Congress.

Exercise 9   1 List the similarities and differences between the two parties.

Similarities	Differences

2 Why is there often a Republican President and a Democratic-dominated Congress?

THE FEDERAL JUDICIARY

The chamber of the Supreme Court

In the federal system there are 90 **District Courts** presided over by a district judge, which hear criminal cases involving breaches of federal law and civil cases on federal matters (disputes between states, non-payment of federal taxes, etc). Appeals can be made to the United States **Court of Appeals**, where an appeal is heard by three judges, although in very important cases all nine appeal judges sit together. In the vast majority of cases this court's decision is final and sets a precedent for future cases, although this precedent is not always binding on the Supreme Court.

Although not explicitly given the power of **judicial review** – the power to decide whether the actions of the President, Congress or state governments violate the Constitution – this is the important role that the **Supreme Court** has developed in the legal system. The Supreme Court judges, of whom there are normally nine (though Congress may alter this number) are nominated for life by the President after being approved by the Senate.

Exercise 10 Say whether the following statements are true or false. Correct any false statements to obtain a summary of the passage.

1 The Federal courts only deal with important crimes.
2 All final appeals go to the Supreme Court.
3 The Supreme Court's most important role is that of judicial review.
4 Judicial review gives the Supreme Court the power to decide that an action of the President is illegal.

STATE GOVERNMENT

There is very little in the Constitution about state government – the Tenth Amendment (1791) merely says that those powers not specifically delegated to the federal government are reserved for states. While the fifty state constitutions differ widely, they all include **the separation of powers** and a system of **checks and balances**, and share the underlying American belief that government should be kept to a minimum. Each state has a **Governor**, a **Legislature** and a **State Judiciary**. The Governor is elected directly in a state-wide election. All the states except Nebraska have bicameral legislatures, normally called the Senate and House of Representatives.

The judicial systems of the states vary greatly in structure and procedures. Generally speaking, however, at the lowest level there are Justices of the Peace Courts, presided over by elected lay magistrates, which deal with minor offences. Then come the County Courts, which deal with the majority of civil and criminal cases. Appeals go to the District Court of Appeals, while the State Supreme Court has the same role as the United States Supreme Court in the federal system. The most controversial aspect of state judiciaries is that in more than two-thirds of the states judges (including those in the Supreme Court) are elected.

Exercise 11 Complete the following sentences to obtain a summary of the text.

1 All the state constitutions are based on . . .
2 And in every state there is . . .
3 Nebraska is the only state which . . .
4 A controversial aspect of most state judiciaries is that . . .

American institutions

THE MEDIA

The First Amendment to the Constitution prohibits Congress from making any law that interferes with the freedom of the press and this freedom has been vigorously defended. The media indeed have uncovered and made public many secrets the government would have preferred to keep secret (such as the Watergate scandal), leading to constant tension between journalists and government officials. Some people say that the media – and television in particular – have become so influential that in effect they are the political process, shaping public opinion.

The Press

Although there are two American news services operating worldwide – the Associated Press (AP) and United Press International (UPI) – the tremendous size of the nation, the variety of time zones, and the general preoccupation with mainly local issues make it difficult for national daily newspapers to exist. An attempt has been made to introduce the 'popular' *US Today* on a nationwide basis, and *The Wall Street Journal* comes close to being a national newspaper. *The New York Times*, with a circulation of 900,000, is perhaps the most influential daily newspaper, followed by the *Washington Post* and *The Los Angeles Times*. All large American cities have at least one newspaper and, although largely concerned with local affairs, they are also read in other states. Periodicals exist for virtually every type of interest, some with just a tiny circulation, others like *Time* with a circulation worldwide of more than 6 million copies. More than 50 of the leading magazines produce over one million copies of each issue.

Exercise 12 List the reasons why there are no real national daily newspapers in the US.

Television and radio

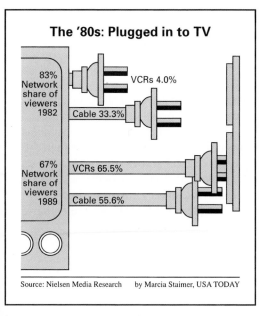

The '80s: Plugged in to TV

83% Network share of viewers 1982

VCRs 4.0%

Cable 33.3%

67% Network share of viewers 1989

VCRs 65.5%

Cable 55.6%

Source: Nielsen Media Research   by Marcia Staimer, USA TODAY

Over 98% of American homes have television sets, and there are more than 900 commercial television stations. More than 600 of these are affiliated with the big three private national television networks, **ABC**, **NBC** and **CBS**, which show their programmes at the same time throughout the nation during **prime time** (the hours in which most people watch television – usually 7.30 pm to 11 pm). The rest are either independent or in smaller networks. An increasing number of Americans also subscribe to cable television stations. There is no national radio station in the United States, but every large city has dozens of independent stations, which range from twenty-four hours a day news to rock and classical music.

Exercise 13 Say what changes occurred in the 1980s in relation to TV viewing.

EDUCATION

Education is not mentioned in the Constitution, nor is there any federal department of education, so the matter is left to individual states. Education is free and compulsory in all states, however, from the age of 6 till 16 (or 18).

At 6 years of age children begin the first year of **elementary school**, which is called **grade 1** or **first grade** (the second year is 'grade 2', etc). At elementary school the emphasis is placed on the basic skills (speaking, reading, writing and arithmetic), though the general principle throughout the American school system is that children should be helped and encouraged to develop their own particular interests.

Graduation Day at an American high school

Children move on to **high school** in the ninth grade, where they continue until the twelfth grade. There are two basic types of high school: one with a more academic curriculum, preparing students for admission to college, and the other offering primarily **vocational education** (training in a skill or trade). The local school board decides which courses are compulsory. There is great freedom of choice, however, and an important figure in high schools is the **guidance counsellor**, who advises the students on what courses to take on the basis of their career choices and frequent aptitude and ability tests.

In order to receive the **high school diploma** necessary in most states to get into college, students must accumulate a minimum number of **credits**, which are awarded for the successful completion of each one- or half-year course. Students hoping to be admitted to the more famous universities require far more than the minimum number of credits and must also have good **grades** (the mark given on the basis of course work and a written examination). Extra-curricular activity (such as playing for one of the school's sports teams) is also very important in the American school system and is taken into consideration by colleges and employers.

Exercise 14   Answer these questions to obtain a summary of the text.

1 Who is responsible for education in the US?
2 At what age do students start elementary school?
3 What type of school comes after elementary school, and at what age?
4 Who decides what subjects students study at school?
5 What do you need to obtain the high school diploma?
6 Is sport important in the American school system?

Exercise 15　In American schools the students are assessed throughout the year by means of multiple-choice tests. In November 1989 the newspaper *USA TODAY* printed some of these tests for parents and children to do together. Below is a selection of questions suitable for students in the 12th Grade. Do the test yourself: all the answers can be found in the preceding pages about the USA.

SOCIAL STUDIES GRADE 12

(Numbers in brackets are the percentage of kids of that age who have answered that question correctly.)

1. The major criticism of the U.S. Electoral College systems is: (63%)
   a) it delays the selection of a winner in presidential elections
   b) it encourages the growth of third parties
   c) it permits a candidate to be elected president without a majority of the popular vote
   d) it undermines the power of political party conventions

2. The First Amendment to Constitution guarantees: (64.5%)
   a) the right to vote
   b) the right to an education
   c) freedom of religion
   d) freedom from slavery

3. The term 'separation of powers' refers to the: (69.1%)
   a) state powers and duties not given to the central government
   b) division of authority among legislative, judicial and executive branches of government
   c) division of a legislature into two houses
   d) creation of a national capital that is not part of any state

4. How many United States senators does each state have? (59.8%)
   a) 1
   b) 2
   c) 3
   d) The number varies according to a state's population

5. The chief justice of the U.S. Supreme Court is selected by: (65.3%)
   a) a national election with approval by a majority of state governors
   b) a vote of existing Supreme Court justices
   c) constitutional amendment and presidential signature
   d) appointment by the president with consent of the Senate

6. How many representatives does each state have in the U.S. House of Representatives? (61.1%)
   a) 2
   b) 3
   c) The number varies according to the area of a state
   d) The number varies according to the population of a state

7. The powers of Congress are set forth in the: (61.7%)
   a) Declaration of Independence
   b) Articles of Confederation
   c) Constitution of the United States
   d) Bill of Rights

8. Which of the following are elected to office? (55.9%)
   a) Members of the House of Representatives
   b) Directors of government agencies
   c) Supreme Court justices
   d) Members of the President's Cabinet

9. Under the U.S. Constitution, the power to tax belongs to the: (51%)
   a) president
   b) Treasury Department
   c) Supreme Court
   d) Congress

10. What person or group has the authority to decide whether a law is constitutional? (50.8%)
    a) The president
    b) A governor
    c) The Congress
    d) The Supreme Court

11. Which among the following regions of the United States was first to be settled by Europeans coming to America? (46%)
    a) Great Plains
    b) Western Plateau
    c) Appalachian Highland
    d) Pacific Mountains

12. Which of the following may vote in a closed primary election? (43.1%)
    a) All eligible voters
    b) Only registered voters with a party affiliation
    c) Only dues-paying members of a political party
    d) Only elected delegates to a party convention

13. Judicial review is best described as the: (54.9%)
    a) right of Congress to reverse Supreme Court decisions
    b) American Bar Association assessment of the quality of judges' decisions
    c) president's right to review and veto actions of federal judges
    d) courts' authority to decide if government actions are constitutional

14. The first 10 amendments to the U.S. Constitution are called the: (73.2%)
    a) Preamble
    b) Bill of Rights
    c) Articles of Confederation
    d) Separation of Powers

15. What did the United States attempt to do through the Marshall Plan? (54%)
    a) Increase trade with communist countries
    b) Isolate itself from other nations
    c) Rebuild the economies of countries damaged in World War II
    d) Acquire colonies in the Third World

1 Did you score better than the average American student?
2 Discuss the advantages and disadvantages of these multiple-choice tests compared with the oral questioning of students as used in Italian schools.

HIGHER EDUCATION

Students on a US university campus

Graduation Day

There are about 3,000 colleges and universities, both private and public, in the United States. They are all independent, offering their own choice of studies, setting their own admission standards and deciding which students meet those standards. The greater the prestige of the university, the higher the credits and grades required.

The terms 'college' and 'university' are often used interchangeably, as 'college' is used to refer to all **undergraduate education** and the four-year undergraduate programme, leading to a bachelor's degree, can be followed at either college or university. Universities tend to be larger than colleges and also have **graduate schools** where students can receive **post-graduate education**. Advanced or graduate university degrees include law and medicine.

During the first two years students usually follow general courses in the arts or sciences and then choose a **major** (the subject or area of studies in which they concentrate – the other subjects are called **minors**). **Credits** (with grades) are awarded for the successful completion of each course. These credits are often transferable, so students who have not done well in high school can choose a **junior college** (or **community college**), which offers a two-year 'transfer' programme, preparing students for degree-granting institutions. Community colleges also offer two-year courses of a vocational nature, leading to technical and semi-professional occupations, such as journalism.

Exercise 16 Say whether the following statements are true or false. Correct any false statements to obtain a summary of the text.

1 There is no minimum requirement to get into college.
2 Colleges and universities are exactly the same.
3 Students do not specialize in their degree subjects during their first two years at college.
4 Students are awarded credits for successfully completing a course.
5 Junior colleges only offer vocational courses.

Exercise 17 Match the terms below with their correct definitions.

1 community college 2 credit 3 major 4 vocational education

☐ main subject of academic study
☐ training in skill or trade to be pursued as a career
☐ educational institution offering two years of studies that correspond to the first two years of a four-year college
☐ recognition by a college that a student has fulfilled one of the requirements leading to a degree.

American institutions

CHURCHES

One of the reasons for which many of the first immigrants left England and Germany was to escape religious persecution (such as the Puritans and the Mennonites). These immigrants brought with them their own particular brands of Protestantism. This lack of a national religion resulted in religious freedom being explicitly recognized in the Bill of Rights attached to the original Constitution.

The variety of religions increased at the end of the 19th and beginning of the 20th centuries with the massive influx of immigrants from central and southern Europe. Nearly a quarter of the present population are Catholic and there are also about 6 million Jews. The majority of the population, however, belong to one of the 1,000 or so Protestant Churches. A common phenomenon in the United States has been the rise of new Churches or sects, such as the Mormons, Jehovah's Witnesses and Christian Scientists.

Most Churches in America are characterized by a strong evangelical spirit. Nowadays, there are not quite so many preachers travelling around the nation with their bibles, as many preachers make use of television to preach their message.

Exercise 18
1 Why has there never been an official religion in the US?
2 Which is the largest single Church in the US?
3 Which religion do the majority of the population belong to?
4 What features do many of the Protestant Churches have in common?

TRADE UNIONS

The first important national organization of workers was the Knights of Labor, founded as a secret union in 1869. Its main aim was to win shorter hours, higher wages and satisfactory working conditions. Although it had nearly a million members by 1886, its mixture of all different types of workers prevented it from being effective. This led to the creation of the American Federation of Labor (A.F.L.), which was a federation of separate, quite autonomous, craft unions. The growing dispute over whether to organize the unions according to crafts or trades, or on an industrial basis (i.e. incorporating all the workers in a given industry) led to the creation of an independent federation – the Congress of Industrial Organizations (C.I.O.) – in 1938. With the continual increase in mass production and unskilled workers, the A.F.L. also began to organize itself on an industrial basis instead of according to craft. The two organizations then merged in 1955 to found a new federation: the A.F.L.-C.I.O.

Unions have never been able to achieve the same levels of membership as in most other Western countries. The political power of the giant corporations and the laissez-faire basis of the American economy has frequently resulted in restrictive laws being made by Congress and individual states against unions, especially in periods when numerous strikes occur.

Exercise 19
1 What were the main aims of the Knights of Labor?
2 What was the difference between the A.F.L. and the C.I.O.?
3 Why are the unions in the US weaker than in most Western countries?

FEDERAL RESERVE SYSTEM

The Federal Reserve System is a decentralized central banking system used to implement the United States' monetary policy which consists of twelve central banks instead of just one. The country is divided into twelve Federal Reserve Districts, each with its own Federal Reserve Bank (though by far the most important is the Federal Reserve Bank of New York). The system is coordinated and controlled in Washington by a Board of Governors who are appointed by the President. This Board of Governors, sometimes called the Federal Reserve Board, is responsible for general credit policy. It fixes the reserve requirements and the maximum interest on bank deposits, is responsible for the issue of banknotes and determines the discount rate in cooperation with the Federal Reserve Banks. The Federal Reserve Banks, in addition to serving as clearing banks, also act as fiscal agents for the Treasury (collecting taxes, paying interest on government bonds, etc).

It is only compulsory for National Banks to be members of the Federal Reserve System, but about 50% of all the banks in the United States belong to the system. These banks must keep a fixed percentage of their deposits as a reserve with the Federal Reserve Banks.

Exercise 20 Complete the flow chart, and list the functions of the organizations mentioned.

FEDERAL RESERVE SYSTEM

Organization   Functions

┌──────────────────────────┐   1 ....
│   │
│   │   2 ....
│ .... │
│   │   3 ....
│   (in Washington)   │
│   │   4 ....
│   │
│   │   5 ....
└──────────────────────────┘

┌──────────────────────────┐
│   ....   │
│   │   1 ....
│ Federal Reserve Districts │
│   each with its own   │   2 ....
│   │
│   ....   │   3 ....
│   │
└──────────────────────────┘

Exercise 21 Use the completed flowchart to give a brief description of the Federal Reserve System.

WALL STREET

Wall Street itself is a short street in Lower Manhattan, New York City, which takes its name from the town wall built by Peter Stuyvesant in 1653 across Manhattan Island to protect the Dutch colonists of New Amsterdam from both the Native American Indians and the English. Symbolically, however, 'Wall Street' means the **financial centre** of the United States (just as the 'City' of London is the financial centre of the United Kingdom) because of the concentration of business institutions in the area: stock-brokerage companies, banks, trusts, insurance corporations, commodity exchanges (coffee, cotton, metal, produce, corn) and, of course, the New York Stock Exchange.

The NYSE is a voluntary asssociation of about 1300 members who trade in **securities** (stocks and bonds) either on their own account or as brokers for others. The Exchange – sometimes called 'the nation's market place' – was founded on May 17, 1792, when Alexander Hamilton, the first US Secretary of the Treasury, decided to issue government bonds to consolidate and refund the debts incurred during the War of American Independence; a 'market place' for the selling and buying of these bonds became necessary.

Membership of the NYSE was made saleable in 1868. The price of membership has varied considerably over the years: in 1929, just before the Wall Street Crash put an end to the stock-market speculation which had characterized the 1920s, the price reached the enormous sum of $625,000. In 1942, during a recession, it fell to $17,000.

New York Stock Exchange

Originally a 'call market' in which the President of the Exchange 'called off' the name of each stock and brokers made their bids to buy or their offers to sell, in 1871 the NYSE became an **'auction market'** in which stocks are sold to the highest bidder continuously throughout the day.

The Exchange deals only in **'listed' stocks**, i.e. stocks which are on the official trading list of the Exchange. In order to be listed on the NYSE, a company must have at at least 2000 stockholders, with at least 1 million shares distributed among them, and an annual turnover of at least $2.5 million. In 1989, there were 2,250 listed stocks.

A feature of the New York Stock Exchange is the **Dow Jones Average**, statistics which show the average price of stocks and bonds traded on the Exchange. (The UK equivalent is the 'Financial Times Stock Exchange 100-Share Index'.) Computed every trading hour of every business day by Dow Jones & Co., a financial publishing company, the Average shows the average price of the stocks of 30 industrial firms, 20 transportation firms, and 15 utility (service) companies. Movement of the Average is expressed in points (a news report may state, for example, that 'the Dow Jones Average opened this morning at 879.32 points and closed at 882.56 points – a rise of 3.24 points') and is widely regarded – by investors, financiers, and governments – as an indicator of the health of the US economy.

Exercise 22

1 Summarize the history and organization of the New York Stock Exchange.
2 Describe the Dow Jones Average and its importance.

Commercial, economic and political institutions

Most institutions and organizations are known by their initials (e.g. the F.B.I.) rather than their full titles (the Federal Bureau of Investigation). Below is a list of the major commercial, economic and political institutions in the world today.

(Br.) has been used to indicate British institutions; (Am.) to indicate American institutions; (Euro.) to indicate European institutions. All the others are international institutions, or it is obvious from the name itself which country or countries they operate in.

Most of the abbreviations given below have been printed with points (e.g. A.B.C.C.), but you will also see them written without points (e.g. ABCC).

Some of the abbreviations are usually pronounced as words rather than separate letters. In these cases, points are not used, and the pronunciation has been given (e.g. ACAS /'eɪkæs/, not A.C.A.S.).

A.B.C.C.	Association of British Chambers of Commerce
A.C.A.	(Br.) Associate of the Institute of Chartered Accountants
ACAS	/'eɪkæs/ (Br.) Advisory, Conciliation and Arbitration Service
A.C.I.I.	(Br.) Associate of the Chartered Insurance Institute
A.F.L.	American Federation of Labor
AMEX	/'æmeks/ American Stock Exchange
A.S.A.	(Br.) Advertising Standards Authority
A.S.E.	American Stock Exchange
B.A.E.	(Am.) Bureau of Agricultural Economics
B.C.A.	(Am.) Bureau of Current Affairs
B.I.R.	(Am.) Bureau of Internal Revenue
B.I.S.	Bank of International Settlements
B.L.S.	(Am.) Bureau of Labor Statistics
C.A.	Chartered Accountant
C.A.C.M.	Central America Common Market

CAP	/kæp/ (Euro.) Common Agricultural Policy
CARICOM	/'kærɪkɒm/ Carribean Common Market
C.B.I.	Confederation of British Industry
C.C.C.	Commodity Credit Corporation
C.E.A.	Commodity Exchange Authority
C.E.G.B.	(Br.) Central Electricity Generating Board
CHAPS	/tʃæps/ Clearing House Inter-Bank Payments System
C.I.A.	(Am.) Central Intelligence Agency
C.I.I.	(Br.) Chartered Insurance Institute
C.I.O.	(Am.) Congress of Industrial Organizations
COMECON	/'kɒmkɒn/ (Euro.) Council for Mutual Economic Assistance
COMEX	/'kɒmeks/ New York Commodity Exchange
D.T.I.	(Br.) Department of Trade and Industry
E.B.I.	European Bank of Investment

E.E.C.	European Economic Community	LAFTA	/ˈlæftə/ Latin American Free Trade Association
ECU, ecu	/ˈeɪkjuː/ European Currency Unit		
E.C.U.	European Customs Union	L.C.C.	(Br.) London Chamber of Commerce
EFTA	/ˈeftə/ European Free Trade Association		
		L.M.E.	(Br.) London Metals Exchange
E.M.S.	European Monetary System	L.S.E.	(Br.) London School of Economics
E.N.E.A.	European Nuclear Energy Agency	NAFTA	/ˈnæftə/ New Zealand-Australia Free Trade Agreement
E.O.E.C.	European Organization for Economic Co-operation		
		N.A.S.D.	(Am.) National Association of Security Dealers
E.P.U.	European Payments Union		
E.R.M.	(Euro.) Exchange Rate Mechanism	N.B.E.R.	(Am.) National Bureau of Economic Research
EURATOM	/ˈjʊərətɒm/ European Atomic Energy Community		
		N.F.C.	(Am.) National Freight Corporation
EXIMBANK	/ˈeksɪmbæŋk/ Export-Import Bank	N.H.S.	(Br.) National Health Service
F.A.O.	Food and Agricultural Organization (of the United Nations)	N.L.R.B.	(Am.) National Labor Relations Board
F.B.I.	(Am.) Federal Bureau of Investigation	N.Y.S.E.	(Am.) New York Stock Exchange
F.C.A.	(Br.) Fellow of the Institute of Chartered Accountants	O.E.C.D.	Organization for Economic Co-operation and Development
FECOM	/ˈfiːkɒm/ European Monetary Co-operation Fund	O.E.E.C.	Organization for European Economic Co-operation
FED, Fed	/fed/ (Am.) Federal Reserve System; F.B.I.	O.F.T.	(Br.) Office of Fair Trading
		OPEC	/ˈəʊpek/ Organization of Petroleum Exporting Countries
F.R.B.	(Am.) Federal Reserve Bank		
F.T.C.	(Am.) Federal Trade Commission	S.E.C.	Securities and Exchange Commission
GATT	/gæt/ General Agreement on Tariffs and Trade	S.I.T.C.	Standard International Trade Classification
I.A.D.B.	Inter-American Development Bank	S.S.A.	(Am.) Special Security Administration
I.A.T.A.	International Air Transport Association	SWIFT	/swɪft/ Society for Worldwide Interbank Financial Telecommunications
I.B.A.	Industrial Bankers Association		
I.B.R.D.	International Bank for Reconstruction and Development (World Bank)	T.U.C.	(Br.) Trades Union Congress
		UNCTAD	/ˈʌŋktæd/ United Nations Conference on Trade and Development
I.C.C.	International Chamber of Commerce		
I.C.C.H.	International Commodities Clearing House	UNESCO	/juːˈneskəʊ/ United Nations Educational, Scientific and Cultural Organization
I.C.F.T.U.	International Confederation of Free Trade Unions		
I.E.A.	International Energy Agency; (Br.) Institute of Economic Affairs	U.N., U.N.O.	United Nations (Organization)
		U.S.E.S.	(Am.) United States Employment Service
I.G.C.	(Euro.) Inter-governmental Conference	U.S.T.C.	United States Tariff Commission
I.L.O.	International Labour Organization	W.F.T.U.	World Federation of Trade Unions
I.M.F.	International Monetary Fund	W.H.O.	World Health Organization (of the United Nations)

The English language

THE HISTORY OF ENGLISH

When the Angles and Saxons invaded Britain in the 5th century A.D., they brought with them their language: 'Englisc' or, as we call it now, **Old English**. Examples of Old English words are: *sheep, dog, work, field, earth, the, is, you*. Two hundred years later, when St. Augustine brought Christianity to Britain in the 7th century, hundreds of Latin and Greek words were adapted into Old English: words such as *hymn, priest, school, cook*. In the 8th, 9th and 10th centuries, the Viking invaders added their own Norse words: *get, wrong, leg, want, skin, same, low*.

When the Norman Duke William defeated the Anglo-Saxon King Harold at the Battle of Hastings in 1066 and became King William I, French became the language of the educated classes for the next two or three centuries. This meant that there was no conservative influence on the English language, which was spoken mainly by uneducated people, and so the **Middle English** period (1150–1500) was characterized by tremendous changes. Grammatically, most of the inflections or case endings of Old English disappeared, and word order therefore became of prime importance, as it is in modern English; at the same time, there was a massive transfer of French words into English (some estimates say over 10,000 words). Latin, however, remained the language of the church and of education, and this mixing of Latin, French and native English is the reason why there are so many synonyms even today in the English language, e.g. *ask* (English), *question* (French), *interrogate* (Latin); *time* (English), *age* (French), *epoch* (Latin).

The introduction of the printing press in about 1476 gave rise to the need for a standard, uniform language that could be understood throughout the country. **Modern English** may be said to have begun in 1500, and the most important influence on the language was William Shakespeare, who proclaimed in *Love's Labour's Lost*, that: 'Henceforth my wooing mind shall be expressed/In russet yeas, and honest kersey noes', i.e. that 'pure' English was the language in which Englishmen best expressed themselves.

Exercise 1
1 List the languages that have had an important influence on English.
2 What is the main grammatical difference between Old English and Modern English?

THE SPREAD OF ENGLISH

English was exported to Britain's growing number of colonies, which by the 19th century accounted for one quarter of the world's population. In the 20th century, even though Britain's role as a world power has declined considerably, the hegemony of the USA has meant that the English language has almost achieved the status of a **world language**. It is estimated that one in five people in the world speak English – 300 million as their first language; 600 million as a second or foreign language; 1 million as a foreign language.

Exercise 2 In the countries listed in the table, English is used either as a first language or as a second language. Identify the 7 countries in which it is used as a first language.

Australia	Ghana	Malaysia	South Africa	Zambia
Bangladesh	Hong Kong	New Zealand	Tanzania	Zimbabwe
Canada	India	Nigeria	Trinidad	
Cameroon	Irish Republic	Pakistan	Uganda	
Ethiopia	Jamaica	Philippines	United Kingdom	
Gambia	Kenya	Sierra Leone	United States	

VARIETIES OF ENGLISH

As English has spread, so has it changed, and there are now several recognized **varieties of English**. While the English spoken in Britain's former 'white' colonies – the United States, Canada, Australia and New Zealand – is still very similar to British English, and differs from it only in matters of vocabulary and phraseology, the English spoken in the West Indies and in countries such as India where English is the second language can be very different in syntax and grammar.

American English, for example, has been influenced by American Indian languages, by Spanish, and by the languages of all the ethnic groups that have emigrated to the US over the years. But it still understood without difficulty by speakers of British English. Indeed, many 'Americanisms' – words or phrases which originated in America – have been assimilated back into British English; words such as *skunk* (American Indian), *canyon, banana, potato* (Spanish) or expressions such as *to take a back seat, to strike oil, to cave in*. Other words – *automobile, cookie, crazy, highway, mail, movie, truck* – still have an American flavour but are increasingly used by speakers of British English. A few words – *faucet* (tap), *candy* (sweets), *fall* (autumn), *gas* (petrol) – remain decidedly American, as do some forms of spelling (*color* – colour, *theater* – theatre, *tire*, – tyre).

Australian English also has its own 'home-grown' words, some of which have made their way into international English (*boomerang, budgerigar*), though others (*cobber* = friend, *sheila* = girl, *tucker* = food, *dinkum* = good) remain distinctively Australian.

Acknowledgements

The publishers are grateful to the following for permission to use copyright material as indicated in the text and as follows:

The Bank of England (p.50); *Early Times* (pp. 33, 45); *The Guardian* (pp. 7, 38); *The Independent* (p. 4); *The Indy* (pp. 14, 37, 77); Her Majesty's Stationery Office (pp. 6, 11); Penguin Books USA Inc. (p. 64 from *The Free and the Unfree* by Peter Carroll and David Noble, copyright © 1977, 1988 by Peter N. Carroll and David W. Noble, reprinted by permission of Viking Penguin, a division of Penguin Books USA Inc.); *The Sunday Correspondent* (p. 39); *The Sunday Telegraph* (p. 48); TIME Magazine (p. 54); USA TODAY (pp. 51, 53, 58, 85, 87)

The publishers would like to thank the following for their permission to reproduce photographs:

The British Library; The Trustees of The British Museum; Ann S.K. Brown Military Collection, Brown University Library; Coke Estates Ltd; Format Partners; FPG International; Sally & Richard Greenhill; Susan Griggs Agency; Guildhall Library, City of London; Michael Holford Photographs; The Hulton Picture Company; Hulton-Deutsch; Ironbridge Gorge Museum; The Kobal Collection; The Mansell Collection Ltd; The Museum of London; National Portrait Gallery; Network Photographers/Lowe; Pictor International Ltd; Pictorial Press Ltd; Popperfoto; The Press Association; The Science Museum; Science Photo Library/Richard Folwell/Martin Bond; Sygma; The Telegraph Colour Library; Zefa Picture Library (UK) Ltd.